PEARLS AWAITS THE TIDE

Other *Pearls Before Swine* Collections

Floundering Fathers
I Scream, You Scream, We All Scream Because Puns Suck
Stephan's Web
I'm Only in This for Me
King of the Comics
Breaking Stephan
Rat's Wars
Unsportsmanlike Conduct
Because Sometimes You Just Gotta Draw a Cover with Your Left Hand
Larry in Wonderland
When Pigs Fly
50,000,000 Pearls Fans Can't Be Wrong
The Saturday Evening Pearls
Macho Macho Animals
The Sopratos
Da Brudderhood of Zeeba Zeeba Eata
The Ratvolution Will Not Be Televised
Nighthogs
This Little Piggy Stayed Home
BLTs Taste So Darn Good

Treasuries

Pearls Goes Hollywood
Pearls Takes a Wrong Turn
Pearls Hogs the Road
Pearls Gets Sacrificed
Pearls Falls Fast
Pearls Freaks the #%# Out*
Pearls Blows Up
Pearls Sells Out
The Crass Menagerie
Lions and Tigers and Crocs, Oh My!
Sgt. Piggy's Lonely Hearts Club Comic

Gift Books

Friends Should Know When They're Not Wanted
Da Crockydile Book o' Frendsheep

Kids' Books

Suit Your Selfie
When Crocs Fly
Skip School, Fly to Space
The Croc Ate My Homework
Beginning Pearls

Stephan Pastis

A *Pearls Before Swine* Treasury

Andrews McMeel
PUBLISHING®

Pearls Before Swine is distributed internationally by Andrews McMeel Syndication.

Pearls Awaits the Tide copyright © 2021 by Stephan Pastis. All rights reserved. Printed in China. No part of this book may be used or reproduced in any manner whatsoever without written permission except in the case of reprints in the context of reviews.

Andrews McMeel Publishing
a division of Andrews McMeel Universal
1130 Walnut Street, Kansas City, Missouri 64106

www.andrewsmcmeel.com

21 22 23 24 25 SDB 10 9 8 7 6 5 4 3 2 1

ISBN: 978-1-5248-6893-2

Library of Congress Control Number: 2021935771

Pearls Before Swine can be viewed on the internet at www.pearlscomic.com.

These strips appeared in newspapers from October 1, 2018, to March 29, 2020.

Editor: Lucas Wetzel
Creative Director: Julie Phillips
Photographer: Ryan Schude
Cover Design: Donna Oatney
Text Design: Spencer Williams

Production Manager: Chuck Harper
Production Editors: Amy Strassner and Emma Wheatley
Digital Tech: Thang Truong
Assistant: Patricia Alpizar
Lifeguard: Michael Baum

Dedication

**To my best friend, Emilio,
who was so desperate for a friend in first grade that he chose me.**

Introduction

Recently, I went to a memorial service for one of my relatives.

It was a nice memorial, as memorials go, and after the service, everyone gathered in the adjacent church hall.

Soon I was so caught up in conversations with friends and family that I failed to look out the window of the hall. Had I done so, I would have seen news crews from various TV networks.

Now I have some small measure of fame, but I was fairly certain paparazzi wouldn't hound me at a relative's memorial. (Although, I will say here that once, as I was about to carry another relative's casket to the grave, the priest turned to me and said, "Any chance I can ask you to sign something?")

And so I walked toward where the news cameras were set up. And that's when I heard someone whisper:

"Someone stole the body."

Now let me say that of all the things one commonly hears at a funeral ("He was a wonderful man" / "I'll miss him a lot" / "The flowers were beautiful"), it is a bit less common to hear the phrase:

"*Someone stole the body.*"

In fact, I would go so far as to call it a rare occurrence.

So rare that we all went outside to ask what was going on.

And what was going on was that while we were all in the hall, someone had stolen the hearse that was parked just outside.

Now it is difficult to say what exactly goes through a person's mind when he or she decides to steal a hearse.

Perhaps the thought is:

"This will be handy if mom dies."

Or maybe:

"No way a cop will notice me in this."

Either way, someone had decided that stealing a hearse was the wise thing to do.

Which of course sent all of us into a frenzy.

Until we learned the next bit of news.

That our relative's casket was still inside the church. And not in the stolen hearse.

Relieved, we all expected the news crews to just go back to their television studios, for while a stolen hearse was unusual, it was a bit less newsworthy when empty.

But they did not go back to their studios.

And that was due to the next bit of news.

There *was* a body inside.

A *different* body. Going to a *different* funeral.

A fact made clear to the entire social media world when the sheriff's department tweeted out a plea to whomever had stolen the hearse asking him to at least return the body.

Which immediately made me wonder if the driver got a PING on his phone, checked his Twitter feed, and said, "So that's what's banging around back there."

And I don't know about you, but if I were that driver, that's when I'd find the nearest available parking space and just call an Uber.

And soon, there were even more news crews on our church grounds, and news helicopters flying overhead, as sheriff's officers everywhere went in pursuit of the fleeing hearse.

All of which the people at the memorial were trying to process.

But not me. I was more focused on one salient point:

Was the thief taking advantage of the carpool lane?

After all, a person is a person. And there was a second person in that car.

And nowhere on that carpool lane sign that mandates two or more persons does it specify that all of them must be living.

Even more exciting were the possibilities for newspaper headlines, many of which I wanted to offer for free to the news crews around me:

"THIEF FACING STIFF PENALTY"

"REMAINS AT LARGE"

"ABRACADAVER: BODY DISAPPEARS"

But alas, no one wanted help from a cartoonist. For this was a grave situation.

And so the search continued all through the night and into the next morning, when someone finally reported seeing the hearse downtown.

A high-speed chase then ensued, during which the thief no doubt learned that a hearse does not have the cornering capability of a Ferrari.

And ultimately crashed on a freeway.

No word on whether he was using the carpool lane.

Stephan Pastis
October 2021

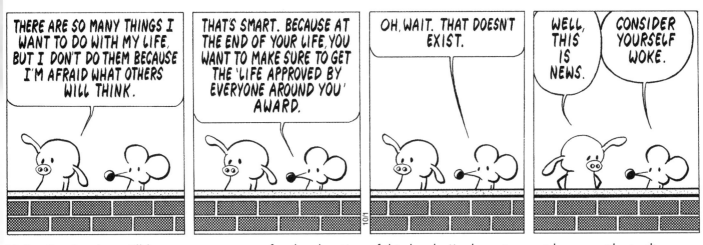

Hello. I'm Stephan. I'll be your commenter for the duration of this book. I'm here to provide you with startling revelations and brilliant insights.

Startling Revelation No. 1: Someone pays me to do this.

That's a car in the second panel. Which you might not know from the drawing itself. Which is the first of many brilliant insights.

11

I know many people around me who adhere to that credo.

I refuse to do chores that are constantly being undone, such as raking. It feels like a waste of my prodigious talents. (My wife, Staci, just walked by as I typed that and said, "Oh, please.")

My wife, Staci, is what kids today call a "hater."

I once lost my driver's license while on a book tour. For every city I flew through, I had to be hand-searched by TSA personnel. Lesson here: If you lose your driver's license, prepare to become very intimate with the TSA guy.

 WHAT ARE YOU WRITING, PIG? / A LIST OF ALL THE STATES I'VE BEEN IN OVER THE COURSE OF MY LIFE.

 OH, HOW FUN...WHAT DO YOU HAVE SO FAR?

 • Emotional wreck • Depressed • Afraid

 WHY IS THAT FUN?

I've been to 41 states. I'm missing Alaska, Wyoming, North Dakota, South Dakota, Iowa, Nebraska, Delaware, Vermont, and Maine. So if you own a large home you're not using in one of those states and the refrigerator is stocked with beer, please feel free to invite me.

 HEY, LOOK, IT'S JOJO JOURNALIST. HE TRIES SO HARD TO INFORM PEOPLE, BUT HARDLY ANYONE SEEMS TO CARE ANYMORE. / YEAH, AND FOR SOME REASON, HE LOOKS REALLY FAMILIAR.

 GOOD GRIEF. / DON'T FALL FOR THE FOOTBALL TRICK!

If you're thinking that Charlie Brown looks really, really good, that may have something to do with the fact that someone I know just scanned it straight out of a *Peanuts* book.

 YEARS AGO, IF I WANTED TO HAVE MY IDEAS HEARD, IT WAS HARD BECAUSE AN EDITOR WOULD HAVE TO AGREE TO PUBLISH THEM.

 BUT THEN CAME THE INTERNET, AND WE ALL SUDDENLY HAD A VOICE.

 It may be just a rumor, but it sounds true to me / You're just saying that because he's black, you racist / Just BOYCOTT his @##!! / It's the worst season anyone has ever made on TV / Who gives a $#@% what you think, fool / Die, $%#$

MAYBE EDITORS WERE GOOD.

This is how I get through life.

Snacks in hotel mini-bars cost about nine times the cost of regular snacks, a fact I conveniently forget when I'm drunk late at night and hungry.

I wear a watch that is broken, just so that when someone points to my watch and asks what time it is, I can say, "It doesn't tell time." To which they say, "So why do you wear it?" And I can answer, "I don't know."

My wife, Staci, said she liked this strip. So she is not always a hater.

Lately I've been experimenting a lot more with strips drawn by one of the characters. It allows me to do jokes that otherwise might not fit within the regular structure of the strip.

The tree revealed in the second panel appears to be dead, giving Rat's statement a subtle reinforcement. Which I didn't notice until now. One of these days I'd like to do something smart intentionally.

I never thought there was such thing as bad pizza until I went to Italy, the birthplace of pizza, and found I didn't like the pizza. Life is cruel that way.

I recently had to clean out the refrigerator in my dad's apartment and found food items that were almost as old as me. Some had grown sentient and wept over being discarded.

The pizza here tasted good because it was not made in Italy. Oooh, snap.

19

After six beers, the seventh really does feel like the right thing to do.

I do this whenever I want to get off the phone with someone. Which I can tell you because I don't think you and I will ever talk on the phone. Though if we do, forget I said that.

 Percentage of my problems that occur during my waking hours:

 100%

 Percentage of my problems that occur when I am asleep in bed:

 0%

 BED IS MATHEMATICALLY CORRECT.

 WHERE ARE YOU OFF TO, RAT? / PIG ASKED IF I WANTED TO TAKE THE FERRY WITH HIM.

 THE FERRY? I DIDN'T KNOW WE HAD FERRY SERVICE. / ME NEITHER.

 YOU NEED TO BE A LOT MORE SPECIFIC.

Surely that's the homeliest fairy anyone has ever committed to paper.

 HEY, OLD WOMAN WANDA, RAT SAYS YOU'VE BEEN COMPLAINING TO THE POLICE ABOUT SOME OF THE STUFF YOU'VE SEEN GOING ON AT OUR HOUSE. / YOU BET I HAVE AND WILL CONTINUE TO. WHY?

 BECAUSE IT'S CURTAINS FOR YOU.

 PRETTY LACY ONES TO COVER YOUR WINDOWS!

 MAYBE I'LL JUST LEAVE THEM ON THE PORCH.

I don't know how I managed this, but this strip is missing the dot shading. Instead of taking responsibility, I will blame my editor, Reed Jackson. Send him your complaints at: Reed Jackson Screwed the Pooch, c/o Andrews McMeel Universal, 1130 Walnut Street, Kansas City, MO 64106.

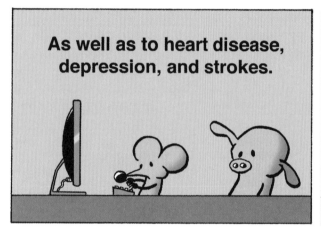

I, Stephan Pastis, invented the use of the phrase "oompa loompas" to refer to a man's testicles. It ranks just above my kids as my proudest achievement.

My son, Thomas, just read the previous comment and reminded me that when I die, my money will go to him, and he will use a good chunk of it to buy *Family Circus* books.

That was out of line.

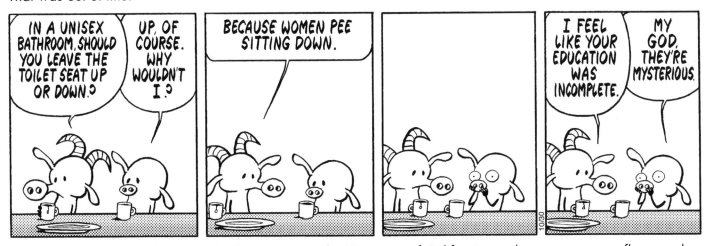

I lived in a coed dorm during my freshman year at the University of California, and everyone on my floor used the same bathroom. So revelations like this came fast and furious.

I cannot believe I got away with this.

In doing these sketchier strips, I think I was influenced by the many great webcomics out there like *Cyanide and Happiness*. To me, they feel like doodles you pass in class.

11/4

This was a very popular strip, particularly when I reposted it on Twitter just after the 2020 election.

I have never run a marathon, but I *have* gotten drunk and smoked an entire pack of cigarettes, which, health-wise, surely cancels out one of those marathoners.

When I hear the word "bandwagon," I picture the Beatles being pulled along in one of those tiny red wagons.

A lot of people seemed to like this strip. Which you have no way of verifying. So I feel free to say it.

I am a FOFO sufferer.

27

My son absolutely cringes when I try to use slang like this. First, because I'm always five years too late. And second, because I threaten to do it around his friends.

Everything I said in that last comment is true. Just keeping it 100, bruh.

There's a rule in our house that if you bend over to pick something up, any other family member can kick you in the rear. Well, maybe it's not a rule. But I enforce it anyway.

Rat's Chart of the Factors That Control Your Destiny...

HARD WORK!

This strip took very little time to draw. I used the extra time to kick family members in the rear.

I DON'T GET IT. I BUY THINGS, THINGS, THINGS, AND I'M NOT HAPPY. SO I BUY BIGGER THINGS, BETTER THINGS, FASTER THINGS, AND I'M STILL NOT HAPPY.

MAYBE LIFE IS ABOUT EXPERIENCES!

I HATE IT WHEN HE DOES THAT.

HELP! HELP! SOMEONE'S HAVING A MEDICAL EMERGENCY! IS THERE A DOCTOR IN THE HOUSE?¿

NO! BUT I'M A NOTARY PUBLIC! AND I CAN SEE TO IT THAT A DOCUMENT GETS SIGNED AND WITNESSED AND I CAN ATTEST TO THE VERACITY OF THE SIGNATURE!

I COULDN'T SAVE HIM.

I wrote this one day after spending an afternoon in a notary's office. Best I can figure, their job is to stare at you and say that you are who you are. I think it's one of the few jobs I could manage.

If I say that I sleep on the left side of the bed, does that mean *my* left when I'm lying in the bed? Or does that mean from the perspective of someone standing at the foot of my bed while I'm sleeping? I'll guess the former because the latter is creepy.

This strip ended up getting reposted on social media by a number of organ donor organizations.

This reminds me of my favorite Groucho Marx quote: "I don't want to belong to any club that will accept people like me as a member."

My plea for the day: Subscribe to your local newspaper. Otherwise, it will go away and you will have no one to give you information when something important happens in your town.

Six Seconds of Your Life You Can't Get Back should be the title of my next *Pearls* book. It accurately describes the daily effect my strip has on others.

WHAT ARE YOU DOING, RAT?

TUESDAY IS 'GIVING TUESDAY'... SO TO HONOR IT, I'M GIVING TO PEOPLE LESS FORTUNATE... HANG ON... I HAVE ONE MORE HOUSE.

WHAT'S THAT?

TUESDAY IS 'GIVING TUESDAY'... SO THERE'S A HUNDRED BUCKS IN THERE.

BUT WHY WOULD YOU GIVE **ME** MONEY?

BECAUSE YOU COULD USE A LITTLE EXTRA CASH, AND WE ALL NEED TO START TAKING CARE OF EACH OTHER.

OH, AND I GOT YOU A NICE CARD, TOO.

PLEASE CONTINUE THE GIVING NEXT YEAR BY GIVING ME BACK THE $100 PLUS 25% INTEREST

I'M GUESSING THERE WAS A CATCH.

LOANSHARKING IS NOT GIVING!!

The first Tuesday after Thanksgiving really is called Giving Tuesday. I don't endorse it. I am, however, in favor of Getting Wednesday, which I just invented.

34

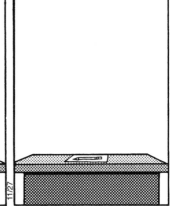

I did this strip after the synagogue shooting that occurred in Pittsburgh, Pennsylvania, on October 27, 2018. I wish there was never a reason to do strips like this.

In the third panel, the towel rack moved mysteriously closer to the scale. I can't explain that.

I really do walk through a lot of graveyards. I enjoy reading the headstones.

12/2

I have one friend who butt-dials me at least every couple weeks. I used to answer, say "hello," and then hang up. But now I just listen in as he goes about his day.

I know for a fact that when they die, perky people go straight to hell.

I couldn't think of anything interesting to say here. So I'm just gonna say that I'm six feet, two inches tall.

In my family, I'm the goofy uncle.

This is an odd one. I think someone must have just hurt my feelings and I put it into a comic strip.

We put our dog to sleep on Wednesday. She had cancer.

Her name was Edee. And she was the only dog I've ever had.

My wife Staci would walk her every morning and stop at this corner where little school kids passed.

Even kids that were afraid of dogs would pet her because Edee was so gentle and sweet. That was her superpower.

PAT PAT

Sometimes when I was drawing, she'd lie on the couch outside my studio door and protect me from squirrels. None ever got me.

(Squirrel free)

zzzzzz

12/9

She also protected me from a mallard duck. It was stuffed and not likely to do much, but Edee's heart was in the right place.

Which is why ours hurt so much now.

So run, Edee, run, to that beautiful field where you always receive the love and affection you gave.

Love, Us

In September 2018, I had to rush to Arizona to help my dad. While I was gone, our dog, Edee, who was already ill, took a turn for the worse, and my wife, Staci, had to have her put to sleep. I knew what time it was going to occur, and so I went to a café in Phoenix and wrote about her as the event was happening. I've never had such a tearstained page.

The strip generated probably the biggest reaction I've ever had to a strip, striking a deep nerve with anyone who has ever lost a pet. We miss you, Edee.

I came up with Franz when I realized how many famous composers had names that could be turned into puns (Lizst, Haydn, Mahler, etc.). And just like that, another annoying character was born.

On the plus side, he's the best dressed of any of my characters.

41

12/16

I wanted to make these pancakes "scratch and sniff" but it is apparently much too expensive.
So please go make your own pancakes and shove them under your nose as you read this.

From the Department of Ridiculously Ironic Ironies: I was working in our yard the other day and met our next-door neighbor for the first time. His name: Bob.

I live about an hour north of San Francisco, where it never snows. But we had one day a few years back where we got something that seemed an awful lot like snow. (I think it was just hail, but what do I know, I live in California.) So I quickly ran outside and made the world's smallest snowman.

43

My wife, Staci, is the one who puts up all the Christmas lights at our house. I contribute not at all to the smooth functioning of our household.

44

I need to bring Franz back. I like him.

One time at a book signing in Ohio, a fan brought me an entire block of cheese. Because I didn't have a knife, I gnawed on the end of it as I signed books. It looked pretty classy.

It really is a creepy line. Even for Santa.

Goat here is based on my wife, Staci, who gets up every morning at around 4 or 5 a.m. She's not right in the head.

Strips that involve gun violence often trigger complaints from people who say that there is nothing funny about the topic. That makes me think twice about doing it.

Oh, I guess I was wrong in my last comment above. What I meant to say was that complaints make me think about doing it twice as often.

When I travel, I often do so alone, which means eating alone. Which probably isn't that surprising given that comment I just made about my wife.

My biggest fear in life is not public speaking, or snakes, or heights. It is dancing in front of other people.

I have thrown many a package against a wall in hopes of getting the impossible-to-open plastic wrapping to magically burst open.

I generally like to avoid identifying specific years in the strip because I think it dates the strip too much going forward. But sometimes it can't be avoided.

I sometimes draw these sad faces on the ends of my pencil erasers. Then I look over at my cup of pencils and get the sense they're all disappointed in me.

How in the world do monocles stay in place and not fall to the ground? Seems like a problem I don't need. I lose even normal glasses.

50

It really would be rather amazing to see people walking around with spears.

"Spatula" is just one of those words that I think is inherently funny.

51

MY PHONE NOW HAS THIS WEIRD START-UP MESSAGE WHEN I TURN IT ON. I THINK IT'S BEEN HACKED BY THE RUSSIANS.

EVERYONE ALWAYS BLAMES THE RUSSIANS. BUT HOW WOULD YOU EVEN KNOW?

COMRADE! EAT BORSCHT!

THEY SHOULD HIDE THEIR TRACKS BETTER.

Hullooo zeeba neighba... Leesten... Me reading biology. And me learn we is different specie.

For you to live, you got eat grass. For me to live, me got eat you. Nature have name for dis.

'Bad news for you.'

I'M CLOSING THE DOOR NOW.

Hey. Me not make rules.

FRANZ, THE PUNNING PROFESSOR OF MUSIC! WHAT DO I HAVE TO DO TO KEEP YOU AWAY FROM THIS HOUSE? BUILD A MOAT?

OH, THAT WOULD BE QUITE THE EYESORE.

FINE... I'LL DECORATE IT WITH ARTWORK. WOULD YOU LIKE THAT?

DEPENDS ON THE MOAT'S ART.

YOU MAKE 'APARTMENT 3-G' LOOK HILARIOUS.

When I was in Vienna, Austria, last year, I went to Mozart's house. Spoiler alert: He's dead.

The alarm on my iPhone is the sound of someone playing the harp. So when I wake up, I briefly think I've died and gone to heaven.

Panel 1: New Year's Resolutions — This year I will worry less.*

Panel 2: WHAT'S THE ASTERISK FOR?

Panel 3: * Provided bad things stop happening in the world.

Panel 4: I'M HOPING THIS IS THE YEAR.

This strip became the cover of my 2021 *Pearls Before Swine* desk calendar. And if that's not a smooth sales plug, I don't know what is.

54

The physics of Rat's body makes it such that when he reaches over his head, his arm needs to double in length. My apologies if that disrupts the sense of realism this talking-animal strip otherwise projects.

I am an Airbnb addict. I've stayed in probably 200 or so. And I've really only had three or four bad experiences, none odder than the strange host in Tennessee who spent a full 20 minutes describing each and every one of her many breakfast cereals. "And this here is Frosted Flakes. With Tony the Tiger. It's very tasty. And this here is . . . ." I left and stayed in a hotel.

Once upon a time, there were corrupt local governments.

But they were watched by people paid to investigate stories.

And the bad people were caught.

Then one day an internet appeared. And everything changed.

And now people want their news for free.

FREE FREE FREE FREE

So there is no one left to watch local government.

MAYOR'S OFFICE

But that's okay, because governments will be good now.

Tee hee hee.

Giggle giggle

EXCUSE ME WHILE I GO SUBSCRIBE TO SEVEN NEWSPAPERS.

DIDN'T YOU HEAR HIM? GOVERNMENT IS GOOD NOW!

This got a very big reaction from various journalists, most of whom perform a really valuable public service.

See, that's how I dance. Which is why I don't do it in front of live humans.

This strip is dated January 16. Which I'd just like to point out is my birthday. Send your generous gifts in the form of cash and checks to Reed Jackson—Don't Steal This to Buy Booze, c/o Andrews McMeel Universal, 1130 Walnut Street, Kansas City, MO 64106.

I saw a stat recently that only 23 percent of people who buy memberships actually use the gym on a regular basis. And when I say "I saw a stat recently," I mean I just looked it up on the internet to have something to say here.

I really do wonder if this happens to the people who make Spam.

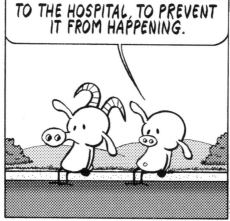

The parents' callousness toward their own kids really makes me laugh.
That probably says bad things about me.

This was a really popular strip.

I rarely block people, but I do mute a lot of them. It's better than blocking because people don't realize you've done it to them.

Rat is probably the character I enjoy writing for the most.

During the pandemic, there were people actually doing this. They missed flying, so they took flights that simply flew around for a while but didn't go anywhere.

I recently read a book that was all about how trees communicate with one another through their underground root system. For example, if there is a threat to one of them (like a swarm of bugs eating it), the threatened tree sends out signals to the other trees to release chemicals that make them less appealing to eat. Though I believe speaking English is still beyond their skill set.

I love simple strips like this. Generally, the less words the better.

I have never once been helped by a troubleshooting guide. Mostly because I'm too lazy to read them.

Dusting seems like a tolerable-enough activity until you learn that 80 percent of dust is human skin.

This is why I only post silly comic strips. My Twitter account is @stephanpastis.

Once upon a time, there was a faraway place where people only got the news they wanted.

THE SKY IS BLUE. YEP!

THE SKY IS RED. YEP!

This divided everyone. Even families.

I CAN'T EAT WITH HIM. HE THINKS THE SKY IS...

Then one day the Great Bunny O' Wisdom descended from the sky with a shocking revelation.

MEDIA OUTLETS MAKE HUGE PROFITS FROM ONLY CATERING TO THEIR VIEWERS. THIS HELPS ONLY THEM.

So the enlightened people gathered all the partisan TV hacks and locked them in the Great Cube O' Silence.

And we Americans met each other again.

HEY...YOU'RE PRETTY NORMAL.

YOU DON'T HAVE HORNS AND A PITCHFORK.

And we could once again get things done.

THE BILL PASSES.

But alas, there's no Great Bunny and we're all screwed.

NO HAPPILY EVER AFTER?

I LIKE TO END ON A REALISTIC NOTE.

I WISHED HIM INTO EXISTENCE!

That bunny does not look wise. He looks mentally disturbed.

65

Safety tip: Don't throw the whole hot dog or hamburger into your mouth. It won't end well.

This is another strip that I can't quite believe I got away with.

A reader recently emailed to say: "I like your comic strip, overall, but the introduction of 'cyclist Jef' to your strip has always made you seem petty."

Which was disappointing. As I thought I'd proven my pettiness years before.

Here I snuck in the polar bear, Total, from my kids' book series, *Timmy Failure*.

My wife, Staci, has recently started buying me cookies called "Joe-Joe's" from Trader Joe's. I cannot stop eating them.

Something about this strip really makes me laugh. I think it's how calmly the waiter is looking on as Rat reads the note.

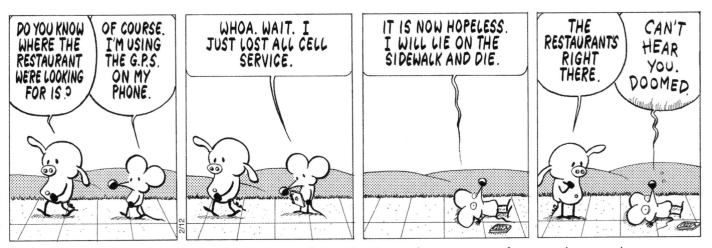

I just checked Screen Time on my phone and it tells me that I spend an average of over six hours a day on my phone. That cannot be right. And if it is, holy $%#$.

The priest of my Greek Orthodox church really is Father Gus, and he gets a kick out of seeing his name in the strip. At least he says he does. Perhaps he's secretly damning me to hell.

As I write this, the pandemic is still in full swing, and trying to pretend that "none of this is happening" has definitely been my coping mechanism.

The only thing more boring than someone telling me all about their trip is someone telling me all about a movie they just watched. Unless it's *Timmy Failure: Mistakes Were Made*. Which I cowrote. So that's fine.

YEARS AGO, I WAS AFRAID TO TRAVEL. FEAR OF FLYING. FEAR OF STRANGE PLACES. FEAR OF STRANGE PEOPLE.

BUT SOON MY CURIOSITY OVERCAME MY FEAR AND I DECIDED TO START TRAVELING.

FROM IRAQ TO BULGARIA... INDIA TO JAPAN... ESTONIA TO PERU. AND EACH TRIP WAS AMONG THE BEST EXPERIENCES OF MY LIFE.

SO WHY DO I BRING THIS UP? SIMPLY TO SAY THAT IN LARGE PART, THAT CURIOSITY WAS INSPIRED BY ANTHONY BOURDAIN.

OOOH

SO IF YOU, LIKE ME, ARE SAD ABOUT WHAT HAPPENED, GO OUT AND TRAVEL TO THAT PLACE THAT MAKES YOU A LITTLE BIT UNCOMFORTABLE.

MEET THAT PERSON YOU SLIGHTLY FEAR.

AND TRY THAT FOOD YOU'VE NEVER TRIED.

PREFERABLY FROM A FOOD CART... LATE AT NIGHT...

BECAUSE THE PARTS UNKNOWN ARE THE GREATEST TO GET TO KNOW.

BUENO? MUY.

This was my tribute to the former host of *Parts Unknown* and *No Reservations*, Anthony Bourdain, who I wish had lived a whole lot longer. He was a big inspiration for me and a huge part of why I love to travel today.

There are still some people out there who get offended when I use the word "God" in the strip, particularly in certain parts of the country. So I get around it by having Pig just write to the "Powers That Be in the Universe." God, I'm clever.

I am more like Rat in real life, but I strive to be more like Pig.

72

I am sure that whenever I do something like this, there are a certain number of newspaper readers who contact the paper to say that something's wrong with that day's comic page. The thought of that gives me joy.

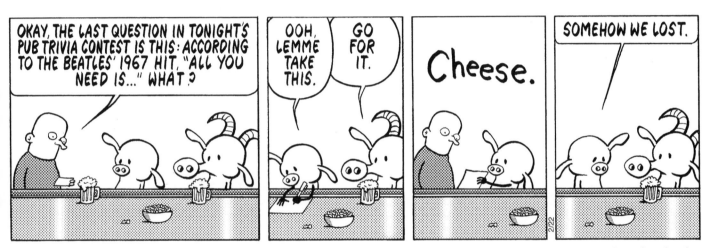

My wife and I recently went to a bar trivia night here in Santa Rosa, California, and lost to some team that had 14 people compared to our five. So really their victory was hollow and nothing to celebrate. Also, I'm not bitter.

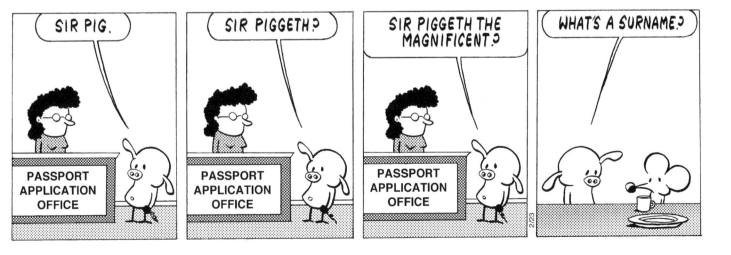

At least his chimney survived.

I am a morning shower person. As are all right-thinking, decent people.

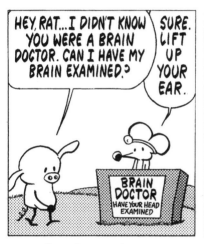

My wife, who is otherwise quite smart, does not excel at spelling. She once spelled "banana" with four n's.

When I check out at the grocery store, I often turn the tabloid magazines around so that you can't see what magazines they are. I know this achieves nothing, but it does make me feel good.

My wife—the same one who cannot spell "banana"—does not like tuna. And while that may not be particularly interesting, it's the only thing I could think of to say here.

This was one of the most popular pun strips I've ever done. Apparently, there are a lot of Queen fans out there.

Pig does not have to take off any clothes to shower. Or put clothes on after. It saves him a lot of time.

To answer Pig's question: the 1970s. My mom sat right next to me, making it harder for me to hide my vegetables in my napkin.

Those are supposed to be actual swear words there. Feel free to guess the words.

Pig's arms are a whopping three times their normal length here, illustrating the point I was making earlier about how the characters' arms have to lengthen when they reach over their heads.

Except me. I am normal and well-adjusted and loved by all.

More Jef strips, more complaints. Including from this woman, who says the Jef strips "further endanger those benign folks who enjoy the sport and/or use it as a necessary means of transportation . . . Instead, maybe some of your humor could be directed at those who harass cyclists for merely 'sharing the road.'"

Nope. Not as funny.

This strip was the result of me living in Portland, Oregon, during the summer of 2018. Many of the trendiest restaurants would not take reservations and didn't care how long you had to wait. I love you anyway, Portland.

So I read *Swann's Way* and can sum it up for you. A guy eats a piece of cake and babbles for the next 512 pages.

81

HEY, LARRY, DOES THIS SKIRT MAKE MY BUTT LOOK BIG?

No.

You butt look big because it big.

Is cold sleeping on porch.

3/14

TODAY IN THE NEWS... ALL THE BAD STUFF THAT HAPPENED YESTERDAY HAPPENED AGAIN.

AND WILL HAPPEN AGAIN TOMORROW.

IF YOU WERE SMART, YOU'D TURN THIS G#*G OFF AND GO STAND IN THE DAISIES.

3/15

I chose daisies because they are the only flower I can draw. Though I suppose sunflowers are within my range.

PIG, GOAT... I'M HERE TO ANNOUNCE THAT I'VE HAD A SPIRITUAL AWAKENING. I AM NOW ONE OF THE FAITHFUL AND WILL BE OBSERVING ALL OF THE RELIGIOUS HOLIDAYS.

3/16

I'M NOT SURE THAT COUNTS.

SAINT PATRICK'S DAY!

Though I'm rather worthless around the house, my wife, Staci, will occasionally send me on Home Depot runs. I rarely buy the right thing. So then she sends me back, this time with a photograph of the item on my phone, so I can show it to someone who works there. One of these days she's going to write my name and phone number on piece of paper safety-pinned to my shirt, in case I get lost.

I've had to totally stop watching cable news at night. I just can't sleep afterward.

I think I'm obsessed with balloons. Maybe it's because when I was a little kid and it was raining outside, my grade school would make us watch a short French film called *The Red Balloon*. It's about a little kid's love for a red balloon, which another kid unceremoniously pops at the end of the film. Good metaphor for what life had in store for us.

This stat is accurate. To the foot, I might add. Depend on me for all your knowledge.

Okay, this is sadly true. I play a ton of *Boggle With Friends*. Some stranger I do not know challenges me every week or so. I have beat him 115 times in a row. And that makes me happier than it probably should.

How come no university has a book as its football mascot? They could call him Bookie and students could place bets with him.

Panel 1:
- Be an astronaut.
- Make a million dollars.
- Write a great novel.

Panel 2:
WHAT ARE YOU DOING, PIG?

LOOKING AT THIS LIST OF GOALS I HAD WHEN I WAS YOUNG AND COMPARING THEM TO MY GOALS AS AN ADULT NOW.

Panel 3:
WHAT ARE YOUR GOALS NOW?

Panel 4:
Survive today.

Panel 5:
IT'S AN AMBITIOUS GOAL.

Panel 1:
HI... ARE YOU, UH, RAT?

YEAH. WHO ARE YOU?

Panel 2:
I'M ONE OF THE JINXIES, AND OUR RECORDS SHOW YOU SAYING, 'THIS WILL BE MY GREATEST YEAR EVER,' BUT NOBODY KNOCKING ON WOOD AFTERWARD.

NO WAIT I

Panel 3:
C'MON, BOYS, MESS UP THIS LIFE!

WHO MADE THAT DUMB RULE?!

If someone around me says something good is going to happen in my life (e.g., "Your book will do great," etc.), I knock on wood three times with both hands. Always three times. Always both hands. Worse, I make the person who said it do the same.

Panel 1:
HEY, GOAT, WILL YOU HELP ME WITH THIS CREDIT CARD APPLICATION?

I'M SURE YOU CAN MANAGE IT YOURSELF, PIG. BUT I CAN DOUBLECHECK IT FOR YOU.

Panel 2:
NAME:
Pig

Panel 3:
SEX:
Only if it's with the right person.

Panel 4:
I WAS OVERLY OPTIMISTIC.

There was a time when it was difficult to say the word "sex" on the comics page. But I think with all that is available for kids to see on just their phones these days, newspapers have become a lot less restrictive.

Panel 1: RAT, WHAT ARE YOU DOING SMOKING AGAIN? YOUR DOCTOR SAID IT COULD REALLY SHORTEN YOUR LIFE.

PUFF PUFF PUFF

Panel 3: CLIMATE SCIENTISTS SAY COMPLETE ENVIRONMENTAL CATASTROPHE MAY BE JUST TWENTY YEARS AWAY

Panel 4: PUFF PUFF PUFF   PUFF PUFF PUFF

My dad used to smoke four packs of cigarettes a day, often in the house. As a result, all of the white baseball pennants in my room turned yellow.

Panel 1: MORNING, PIG. DID YOU HEAR ALL THE STUFF HAPPENING IN THE NEWS? — NOPE.

Panel 2: FOR I AM PROTECTED BY THE WARM BLANKET O' GOODNESS THROUGH WHICH NO TWEET CAN PENETRATE.

Panel 3: PLEASE GET YOUR OWN WARM BLANKET O' GOODNESS.

Panel 1: WHAT ARE YOU WRITING, PIG? — A LIST OF THE PLACES I WANT TO TRAVEL TO BEFORE I DIE.

Panel 2: TERRIFIC! WHAT DO YOU HAVE SO FAR?

Panel 3: Nearest hospital

Panel 4: HOPEFULLY, THEY DRIVE FAST.

I have a book called *1000 Places to See Before You Die*, and I use it to research possible trips. The next places I want to visit are Portugal and Morocco.

For those that might not know it, this pun is based on the Jay-Z lyric, "I got 99 problems, but a bitch ain't one."

From the Facts You Didn't Need to Know Department: When ordering at a café, I always give my name as "Steve." That way, I don't have to spell "Stephan."

I'm often asked why my characters are all left-handed. Believe it or not, it's because it's easier for me to draw the characters facing to their right (our left). As a result, their left arm is exposed, and so they draw with their left hand.

I do occasionally hear from some of my old high school English teachers. They're proud of my smartosity.

I've always wanted to make this joke at a café, but I fear being looked at like the 52-year-old man I am.

This really is the advice experts give in this situation. And not one person has ever listened to it.

One day I want to hear that one of you out there played the numbers given in that second panel. And that you won. And that you're sending me half of all your winnings.

This idea actually originated from an email sent to me by Todd Clark, the creator of the comic strip *Lola* (though his idea was slightly different—he proposed "low spurn count"). He said there was "NO WAY" he could do it in his strip and thus offered it to me. I like that *Pearls* is thought of as the "anything goes" bordello of comic strips.

I get around this by grabbing the handle with the bottom of my T-shirt.

I have never—not once—shattered the screen of my iPhone. And because I expressed that thought, I just knocked on wood three times with both hands.

Another appearance by the polar bear, Total, from my book series *Timmy Failure*.

4/14

From the Department of Snooty Philosophical References You Didn't Need to Know: The old man here is supposed to be Diogenes, a philosopher from ancient Greece who walked around with a lantern searching for one honest man.

Clearly, I saw the plague-filled year of 2020 coming.

1861, for those of you who need to go the bathroom.

This year I made myself watch the entire *Game of Thrones* series. I say "made myself" because I generally avoid anything with elves, wizards, pointy ears, or dragons.

"Only the suck-ups win" would be a great workplace poster.

It's hard for me to draw my own characters badly. So when I do strips like this, I often draw the characters with my left hand.

At least once a year, I still have a nightmare where I am back working as a lawyer and I owe my law firm 20 years' worth of billable hours.

Perhaps the closest I've ever come to using the word "sh*t" on the comics page, if you don't count the time Rat ordered shiitake mushrooms.

   **reptilian**

adjective

deeply disliked,
despised,
repulsive

Whuh you doing, son?

I HAVE TO DO A PAPER ON REPTILES, SO I'M LOOKING IT UP IN WEBSTER'S DICTIONARY.

Oh, yeah. We reptiles greatest guys on earth. Whuh book say?

Typo.

HELLO? BOMBAST CABLE? I'M CALLING TO SAY I'M CUTTING THE CORD. NO MORE CABLE! NO MORE BAD SERVICE! NO MORE OVERCHARGING!

SO SCREW YOU, YOU FOOLS! YOU AND ME ARE DONE! FINISHED! BECAUSE NOBODY NEEDS CABLE ANYMORE! WE HAVE THE INTERNET NOW!!

WE PROVIDE YOUR INTERNET.

THE CABLE COMPANY IS SATAN INCARNATE.

This really is why we still have cable in my family. We need the internet, and they provide both.

THIS FITNESS MAGAZINE SAYS THAT THE KEY TO LOSING WEIGHT IS TO PUT YOUR FOOD ON SMALLER PLATES.

WHY IS THAT?

BECAUSE YOU CAN FILL THE PLATE AND PSYCHOLOGICALLY, IT FEELS LIKE YOU'RE GETTING MORE THAN YOU ACTUALLY ARE.

I'M LOSING WEIGHT.

I believe those are supposed to be hamburgers, hot dogs, and drumsticks in that stack. But even I am not sure.

4/28

My crazy daughter, Julia, gets up at 5 a.m. on Sundays to watch Formula 1 races.
Truly, I am the only sane person in my family.

Regarding that last comment, my daughter would like you to know that she sees me as "THE most unstable loon" in our family. I dispute that.

Speaking of fried foods, I once ate a plate of fried green tomatoes in New Orleans that rendered me unable to eat anything else for three days. I think a grease bomb just exploded in my stomach.

Another example of my comic strip providing solid life advice for the impressionable young children out there.

A newspaper in Indiana printed a letter from a reader saying that this particular strip filled her with "horror" (because the dumb person got killed). But then she went on to say that *Baby Blues* also offended her, so that lowered my street cred.

2019 really was the Year of the Pig. And the very next year (2020) was the Year of the Rat.

Stephan's worst three pizza toppings of all time: (1) anchovies, (2) spinach, (3) olives.

I don't think I've ever seen someone shout "Have my babies" to an author at a book signing. Though perhaps I've been going to the wrong book signings.

This was another legacy of my living in Portland, Oregon, during the summer of 2018. A lot of restaurants listed items that were "sustainably sourced."

Good thing the world never showed us his backside here. Because I'm not nearly as good at drawing Europe and Asia.

For those of you wondering, yes, Rat and Pig have a TV from the 1970s. It's based on the TV in my house when I was growing up. It had four legs and sat on the floor.

And we only had eight channels! ABC, CBS, NBC, PBS, and four local channels. My God, I'm old.

I learned a lot of words from reading *Peanuts* (e.g., psychology, philosophy, grief, etc.). So I sometimes like including words such as "numismatist" because I know kids will look it up and remember it.

I had my airplane tickets booked for Prague when the pandemic hit, and thus the whole trip had to be canceled. I'm hoping to one day still go there and Czech it off my list.

I don't really keep track of when any of the characters' birthdays are. As a result, I'm sure I've referenced multiple dates for each character. Goat alone probably has three or four different birthdays.

I'm fairly certain this is the first comic strip to ever contain the line, "Waiter, there's a fallen shoe in my chai."

In the past, PETA (People for the Ethical Treatment of Animals) has sent me cards thanking me for strips I've done that pointed out the mistreatment of animals. They did not thank me here.

Also, I'm not making up any of these. These were all phrases that PETA proposed changing.

I don't think "bringing home the bagels" quite caught on.

I think this strip would have worked better if the second, third, and fourth panels were combined into just one panel. I think it would have illustrated the rushed time better. Sort of like a kid on a long drive saying, "Are we there yet? Are we there yet? Are we there yet?"

You can always be certain of an upcoming pun if I mention a lot of proper names (Taylor, Burt, Manuel).

That word in the last panel is supposed to be "ass." I could actually indicate that word very clearly if I used the swear squiggles "@$$." But it looks so close to the actual word that I fear some newspapers wouldn't run it.

This strip makes me laugh. Though I'm not sure I needed the cow's line in the last panel. It's funny how often I can see stuff like that only a year after I draw it.

I was a full-time lawyer from 1993 through 2001. Most of the time I worked in downtown San Francisco, but the last couple years I worked in Berkeley.

Somebody I know might have taken the Neighbor Nancy that appears in the third panel and just cut-and-pasted it into the fourth panel. Cartoonists have a phrase for that: lazy turd.

The line in the last panel is a bit unclear. What I meant was that Pig's mom was always giving Pig time-outs. But it can be read that Pig's mom always wrote letters like that to the landlord. So if you're keeping score at home, that's three strips in eight days that I screwed up. Or what the Spanish would call "un fiasco."

6/2

I sleep so much better at night if I turn off all social media. I've even started leaving my phone in the car overnight.

116

Believe it or not, in the 1990s I ran for city council in the town of Albany, California. I came in last. Voters made the right choice.

I think Jef works as a character because a lot of people think that cyclists have that attitude toward them.

This customer typifies me. I go to a café, buy one coffee, then sit there for three hours. I really should pay rent.

When I sit in that same café writing, I often see cyclists come in for coffee, all decked out in their hip-hugging Lycra. And all I can think is, "Oh yeah, I should write another strip about you."

I really do think this is how things are now. People are just tired of other people trying to get them outraged.

"Hoo-haws." Yet another synonym I have created for testicles. I am a pioneer in the field of testicle-naming.

I really like the Comic Strip Censor because he lets me get away with a lot of edgier jokes. No newspaper editor wants to remove the strip that day and risk looking like him.

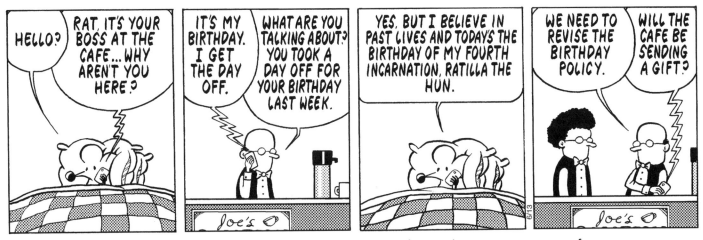

As you know from earlier, my birthday is January 16, and I look forward to your generous gifts.

Rat is the person we all want to be, but know we can't.

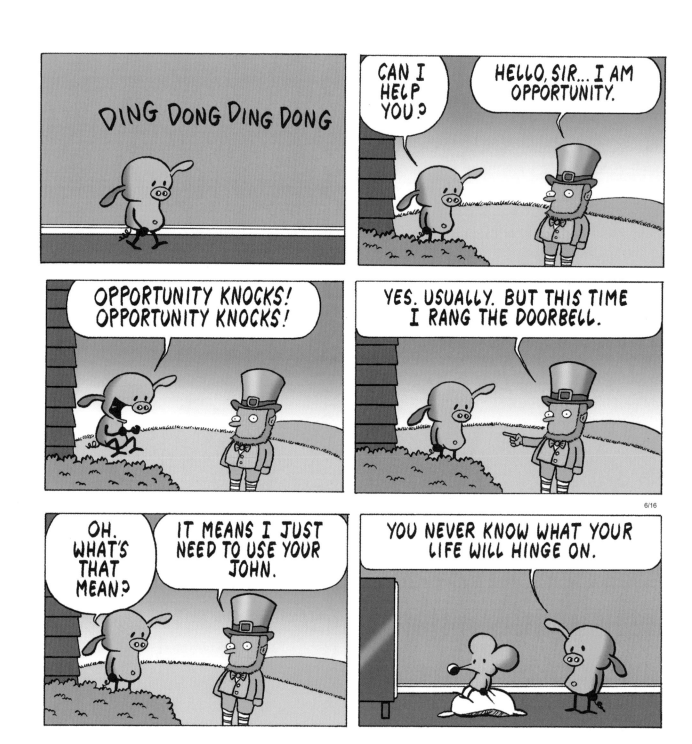

The comic strip *Peanuts* had a bigger influence on me than any other comic strip. And because those characters were always sitting on beanbags when watching TV, I did something similar and had mine sitting on pillows.

When I was a 19-year-old college student in Berkeley, my friends and I used to hop in the car on a Saturday night and drive to Reno, Nevada, to play the slot machines. But because we were underage (and looked it), we had to keep a lookout for casino employees, who would often card us and ask us to leave.

Let me just say right now—that might be the worst drawing of Marvin Gaye ever done. In fact, if Pig didn't announce that's who he was, you'd probably think he was just a short lumberjack.

Some reader once invited me to their book club meeting in order to prove that not all book clubs are boring. I chose instead to watch paint dry.

So my best friend really is Emilio, and we really do play this game. Part of the reason I did this strip was to see how many *other* people actually play this game. And it turns out there are a lot of them.

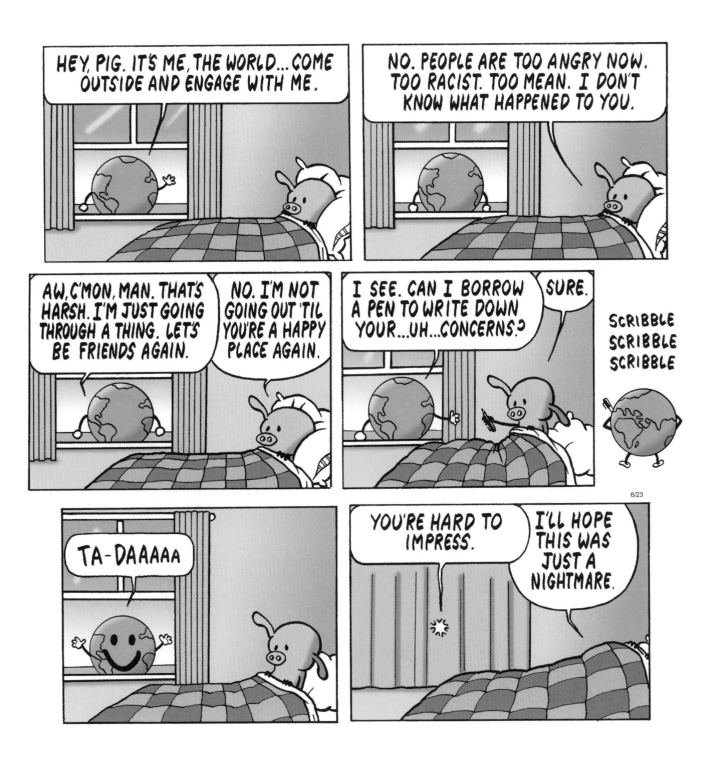

I drew a pretty decent Asia and Africa in the fifth panel, proving that my drawing skills are rapidly improving. Except when it comes to Marvin Gaye. Who I shall never depict again.

WHAT ARE YOU READING, GOAT?

A PHYSICS BOOK. THIS CHAPTER IS ALL ABOUT THE LAW OF CONSERVATION OF MASS.

WHAT'S THAT?

IT'S HOW IN A CLOSED SYSTEM, THE AMOUNT OF MASS CANNOT CHANGE OVER TIME.

WOW. THAT HELPS ME WITH A PAPER I'M WRITING.

GREAT.

Why I'm Still Fat by Pig

I currently weigh 197 pounds. Which you may or may not find fascinating.

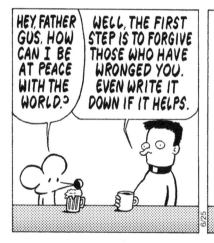   

HEY, FATHER GUS, HOW CAN I BE AT PEACE WITH THE WORLD?

WELL, THE FIRST STEP IS TO FORGIVE THOSE WHO HAVE WRONGED YOU. EVEN WRITE IT DOWN IF IT HELPS.

To those who have wronged me, I FORGIVE YOU.

But just so we're even, let me punch you in the face.

OOH. SO CLOSE.

VENGEANCE HELPS ME FORGIVE.

WHAT'S ALL THIS 'CAP AND TRADE' STUFF I KEEP HEARING ABOUT?

WE CAP THE NUMBER OF IDIOTS AMERICA CAN HAVE AND TRADE THEM TO A COUNTRY THAT DOESN'T HAVE ENOUGH.

OOOH...FREE VACATION.

You can always make fun of idiots because no one reading the strip thinks they're an idiot.

I recently bought my first hybrid, which I believe is a Toyota Avalon. The fact that I am not sure of what my car is shows you how much time I spend thinking about cars.

My wife, Staci, sometimes drops strands of her hair into the dinners she makes for me. She says it's an accident, but I think it's payback for my general uselessness.

I don't believe self-published authors were thrilled with this strip.

Shakespeare reportedly invented 1,700 new words. I'm hoping to catch him and thereby secure my place right next to him in literary history.

Most bunnies are cute. Mine look like Civil War generals with extra-long ears.

There may have once been a bar in Berkeley, California, that college-age Stephan used to go to with his friends late at night because it was often empty and the bartender would disappear into the kitchen and Stephan could fill up his pitcher for free, thereby stealing copious amounts of beer. This is all very hypothetical.

I recently went to a funeral for a family member where, after the morticians dropped off the body at the church, someone stole the hearse. See the story about it in this book's introduction.

Regarding the comment about stealing beer on an earlier page, my syndicate has insisted on adding this note:

The views expressed by Stephan in this book do not represent those of the syndicate or of Andrews McMeel Publishing.

Regarding the syndicate's comment, I would like to add the following comment:

Free beer is good.

On a book tour through Indianapolis, I stopped and toured the Indianapolis Motor Speedway. The track is so big that the infield holds a four-hole golf course.

I recently went through a phase where I read a decent number of books on astronomy. Here is all I can remember:

Some of the stars are blinky.

Goat is the only character who drinks tea, as evidenced by the tea bag string that is generally hanging out of his mug. I think it makes him seem a bit more sophisticated than the other characters.

Woomun! Woomun! Me is catch son do bad tings.

WHAT NOW, LARRY?

He is chase butterfleas.

BUTTERFLIES, LARRY. HE LOVES THEM.

Okay. Dat no Larry son. Larry son grow up, keel tings. Be scary, Larry son no smile, stare at butterfleas.

OKAY, LARRY, GO TELL HIM HOW HE NEEDS TO BE.

Now you tink smart.

JUST KNOW HE WON'T DO IT. INSTEAD, HE'LL GROW UP AND LIVE HIS OWN LIFE. ONLY YOU WON'T BE A PART OF IT BECAUSE HE'LL RESENT YOU.

HAHA HA Now you juss rideeculous.

Larry's love for his son may be his only redeeming feature.

Aww, that's not true. I've gotta be somebody's. Anyone? Anyone?

Fun Fact: Japan gives fathers a little more than six months of paid paternity leave. So if you're a guy living in Japan, have 80 kids and you never have to work again. Other than the part where you raise 80 kids.

There was a tiny little window of my life where I tried to golf. But I was so bad that one time at the driving range, I managed to hit a drive *sideways*, knocking over the bucket of golf balls that the guy next to me was using.

While Amazon is fast and convenient (and I buy a lot of stuff there, too), try to buy books from your local bookstore as well. They're a great resource and are often staffed by really knowledgeable people. Believe me, you don't want those bookstores to disappear.

SURVEY QUESTIONS

Have you chosen to drive a gas-powered vehicle?

☐ Yes ☐ No

If so, do you feel guilty about its effect on the environment?

☐ Yes ☐ No

Do you think your choices in life are in any way related to a poor diet?

☐ Yes ☐ No

If so, do you plan to improve that diet?

☐ Maybe

☐ No

Do you wake up early to exercise?

☐ Not really

☐ No. I'm uninspired.

Will this change?

☐ Hell no

7/21

So what's it like to be a fat, lazy turd?

YOUR SURVEY OF NON-CYCLISTS SEEMS KINDA BIASED, JEF.

PLEASE. WE'RE TRYING TO UNDERSTAND YOUR KIND.

HE DIDN'T ANSWER, 'WHY BOTHER LIVING?'

A few years ago, I realized I wasn't getting in trouble when I used the word "turd" on the comics page. So now I do it whenever possible. That's what I call progress.

DO YOU EVER REMEMBER YOUR DREAMS?

YEAH.

I WAS GONNA BE SUCCESSFUL AND MARRIED AND RICH.

NOT WHAT I MEANT.

YOU'RE REALLY BRINGING ME DOWN.

BEHOLD! A TEST I'VE DEVELOPED TO DETERMINE WHICH OF MY SOCIAL MEDIA FRIENDS I SHOULD CULL FROM THE HERD. I DO IT BASED ON WHETHER THEY POST TOO MUCH, BRAG TOO MUCH, ETC.

OOH, CAN I SEE YOUR TEST?

NO. THE FACTORS I USE TO CULL ARE PROPRIETARY.

LET ME SEE! LET ME SEE!

DON'T TOUCH MY TEST TO CULL!! DON'T TOUCH MY TEST TO CULL!!

COMIC STRIP CENSOR

COMIC CLOSED 'TIL FURTHER NOTICE
Have a wholesome day.

Another testicle reference. Perhaps the 34th in this book. I hope there's a prize for that.

WHAT DO YOU HAVE THERE, RAT?

AN APP I CREATED. TRANSLATES REAL ESTATE AGENT-ESE INTO ENGLISH.

HOW SO?

WELL, THIS LISTING SAYS, 'CHARMING LITTLE FIXER-UPPER.' SO YOU PUT THAT INTO THE TRANSLATOR AND SEE THAT IT MEANS...

JUST SET FIRE TO YOUR MONEY NOW.

IT HELPS TO BE FLUENT.

My wife recently spent way too much on a refrigerator. That comment doesn't fit here, but I just needed somewhere to vent.

MAY
GET
SHOT

Ah, Facebook. You annoying turd.

Addendum to that last comment above: Facebook recently deleted my account on the grounds that I was pretending to be Stephan Pastis. I was really insulted, because if I was gonna impersonate a famous person, I would do a whole lot better than me.

HOW GOOD INVESTIGATIVE REPORTING WORKS

DID YOU DO IT?

I DENY EVERYTHING.

NEWSPAPER INC.

HE'S LYING, SIR... HE DID IT.

WHOA WHOA.. BEFORE WE GO RUSHING TO JUDGMENT, LET'S DO THE LEGWORK ON THIS.

SO REPORTERS FANNED OUT ALL OVER THE CITY.

AND CHECKED AND RE-CHECKED DOCUMENTS.

AND TALKED AND TALKED TO WITNESSES.

AND ARMED WITH FACTS, THEY APPLIED THE WHITE HOT JOURNALISTIC HEAT TO THEIR SUBJECT.

ALRIGHT ALRIGHT. YOU GOT ME! I DID IT!

HOW SOCIAL MEDIA WORKS

DID YOU DO IT?

I—

FOOSH

GUILTY! GUILTY! GUILTY!

I HAVEN'T ANSWERED YET.

SORRY. ON TO THE NEXT THING

SO WHO REALLY NEEDS REPORTERS?

WE DO.

INSTA-JUDGMENT IS SOOO MUCH INSTANT-ER!

For obvious reasons, this was a really popular strip with newspaper reporters.
Also, it's fun to draw flamethrowers.

140

The best way to get in shape is to visualize yourself moving toward your goal.

GOALS

HARD WORK MOUNTAIN GOAL

7/29

I'M SCARED TO GO ANYWHERE THESE DAYS.

YOU SHOULD TALK TO RAT. HE SEEMS TO BE COPING GREAT.

REALLY? WHAT'S HIS SECRET?

BULLETPROOF GLASS BOX.

NOW THIS IS LIVING.

I drew this strip at a time when mass shootings were in the news way too much.

The Adventures of THINKYMAN!

HELP! HELP! Thinkyman! Our country is under attack!

So Thinkyman rushed... To his study... To think... And think.. And think.

City's gone now, Thinky man.

HUSH... Still thinking.

AND THAT'S YOUR SUPERHERO?

AND MEET HIS SIDEKICK... THE PONDERER!

I recently saw my first superhero movie—*Avengers: Endgame*. I had no idea what was going on and fell asleep halfway through. Then I saw that the movie grossed almost 3 billion dollars, apparently proving that I know nothing about anything.

141

The Adventures of THINKYMAN... AND THE PONDERER! By PiG

HELP! HELP! MY FOOT IS STUCK IN THESE ROCKS AND THE TIDE IS RISING!

DO NOT WORRY! WE WILL SAVE YOU!!

BUT FIRST, WE WILL CHECK WITH THE COASTAL COMMISSION TO DETERMINE THE FEASIBILITY OF SAID ACT AND PERHAPS HOLD PUBLIC HEARINGS!

SADLY, HE DROWNS.

THAT DARN COASTAL COMMISSION.

I HEARD YOU FINALLY BEAT YOUR INSOMNIA.

YEAH, I TRIED MEDITATION, COUNTING SHEEP, SLEEP AIDS, BUT NOTHING WORKED. THEN I SUDDENLY FOUND THE SOLUTION ON T.V.

WAS IT A PROGRAM?

YEAH.

WHAT'S IT CALLED?

SOCCER.

SOME PEOPLE APPRECIATE IT.

ARE THEY ALL INSOMNIACS?

I would watch a whole lot more soccer games if the goals were 50 times their current size and the final score was 100 to 98.

HEY, RAT, WHERE'S PIG TODAY?

ON THE COUCH IN THE DEN.

GOSH, HE SPENDS ALL HIS TIME ON THAT STUPID THING. IF HE'S NOT CAREFUL, HE AND THAT COUCH ARE GONNA BECOME ONE.

TOO LATE.

OH, GOD.

IT'S A GOOD LIFE.

I think the Pigcouch could really catch on in the pig-loving community.

Beep
Boop
Beep
Boop
Beep
Boop
Boop

...AT THE TONE THE TIME WILL BE —

TIME LADY! YOU'RE STILL THERE!

YES. WHO'S THIS?

TIME LADY

IT'S PIG. YOU DON'T KNOW ME, BUT I JUST WANTED TO SAY I MISS YOU.

OH. WELL, THANK YOU. YEAH, NOBODY CALLS ME FOR THE TIME ANYMORE. I'M WONDERING IF I DID SOMETHING WRONG.

OH, NO, NO, NO, TIME LADY... IT'S JUST, WELL, WE HAVE PHONES NOW THAT TELL US THE TIME RIGHT ON THE SCREEN.

YOUR PHONES HAVE SCREENS?

TIME LADY

8/4

YEAH, AND A CAMERA, AND IT'S CONNECTED TO EVERYONE AND EVERYTHING.

OH, GOODNESS. WHAT DO YOU USE THEM FOR?

MOSTLY TO TAKE PICTURES OF OUR FOOD AND BE MEAN.

I'M GONNA HANG UP AND EMBRACE THE PAST NOW.

WAIT! TAKE ME WITH YOU!

I wanted to make this woman a regular character, sort of like a connection to the past.
But I never really followed through on it.

143

I think *Sesame Street* would be a better show if it had just a little more violence. Just to make the street a bit more realistic.

Speaking of violence, I have only been in one fight. I threw a dinner roll at a guy and he punched me in the face. Oh well, at least I hit him with a dinner roll.

This is the only *Pearls* strip I can think of that came out looking more like a game of Tetris.

My first syndicate, United Features, did not like me using either the words "crap" or "suck." It was a crappy rule that sucked.

I was a little worried about how this strip would be received, so I hid it on a Saturday, when I always presume less people are reading the newspaper.

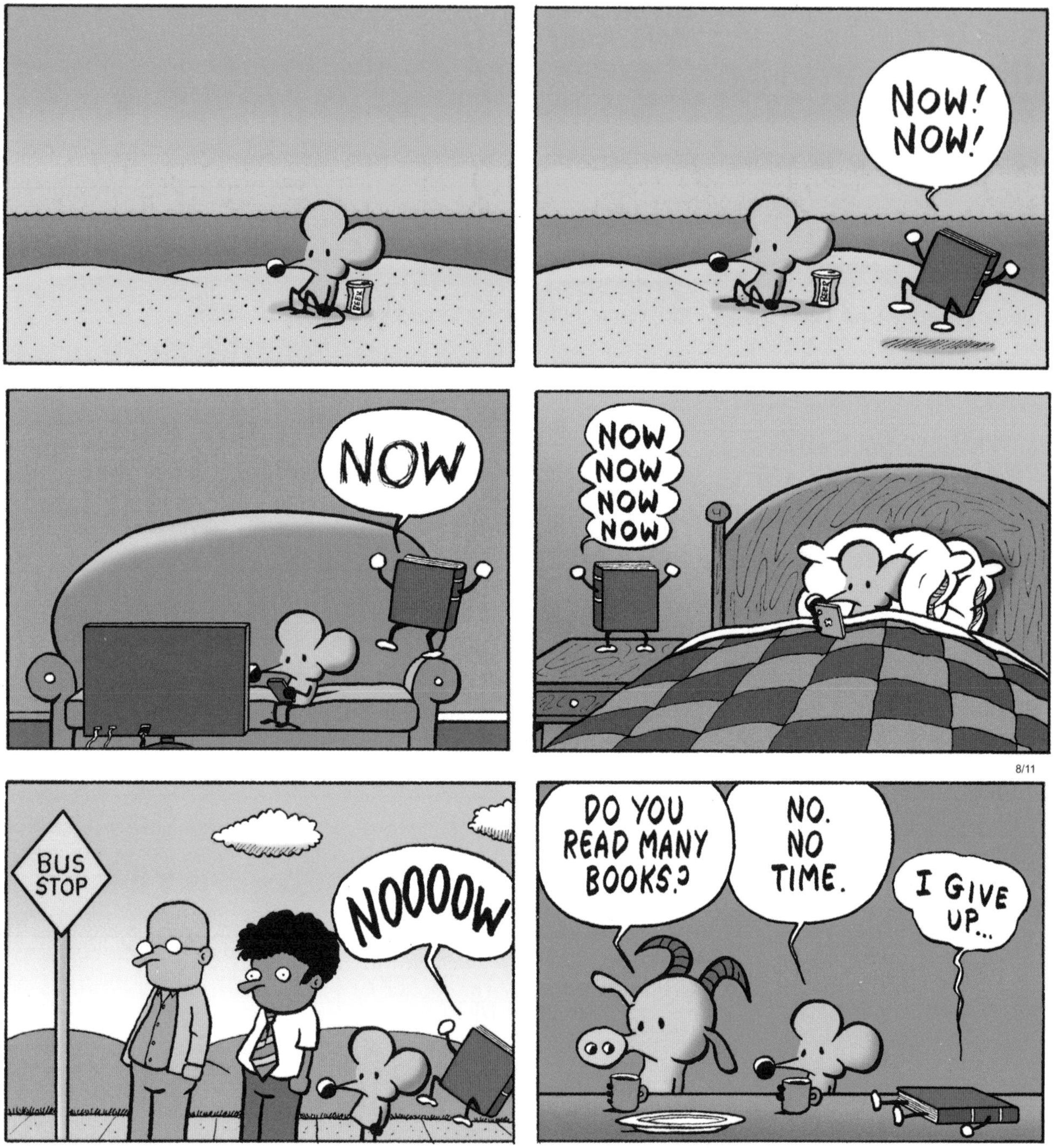
NOW!
NOW!
NOW
NOW
NOW
NOW
NOW
8/11
BUS STOP
NOOOOW
DO YOU READ MANY BOOKS?
NO. NO TIME.
I GIVE UP...

This year I've been trying to read a book a week, which is hard to do. But I've made it easier by choosing kids' picture books that are no more than 12 pages long.

I am apparently obsessed with boxes. If you went back through the 20-year history of *Pearls*, I think you'd find more than 1,000 of them depicted. That is topped only by the number of times I've referenced testicles.

This was a really popular strip. I guess people like to see knife-wielding books. I will suggest that idea to *Sesame Street*.

Pliny the Younger is one of the top-ranked beers in the world. After this strip was published, my wife and I became friends with the owners of the brewery. We even got invited to their house, where they let us try all of their different beers. I asked if I could just move in, but they declined.

This is based on something that actually happened to a friend of mine. He got too close to the bike lane while driving and a cyclist spit on his windshield. Alas, a real-life Jef the Cyclist.

I sometimes find it odd that people are so obsessed with achievements and winning awards.
The rest of the time I'm obsessed with achievements and winning awards.

RAT'S INSPIRATIONAL MESSAGE FOR THE DAY

THERE ARE NO LIMITS TO WHAT YOU CAN DO!

Except your lack of skill. That will stop you cold.

I LIKE TO KEEP PEOPLE GROUNDED.

If I ever stop doing the strip, I know I can always get a job writing motivational posters.

WHAT ARE YOU DOING, PIG?

STUDYING AN ADMINISTRATIVE MAP OF LOUISIANA FOR MY GOVERNMENT CLASS.

OH, YEAH? WHAT HAVE YOU LEARNED?

WELL, THE MOUTH OF THE MISSISSIPPI IS RIGHT HERE. SO I'M WONDERING IF IT FLOODS, WHAT HAPPENS TO THIS COUNTY AND THIS COUNTY.

PARISHES.

THAT POOR COUNTY.

NEVER MIND.

HEY, SLOW-TALKING SAL. HOW GOES IT?

I... GOT... LAID

...OFF.

YOU'RE SHORTENING MY LIFE.

COMIC STRIP CENSOR

For a strip that appears in a lot of newspapers, this one was pushing it. Really, really pushing it. But hey, I'm still here.

I was gonna say something about this strip but now I can't remember what it was.

My wife, Staci, recently went through my sock drawer and threw out every sock that had a hole in it. I didn't even get a chance to say goodbye.

Silly Instagram. That said, I'm on Instagram.

Panel 1: Dear World, Please stop picking on me.

Panel 2: Seriously. There are seven billion other people.

Panel 3: Surely with Google Maps you can find one.

Panel 4: SOMETIMES THE WORLD JUST GETS LAZY.

The ink-staining that happens to Pig when he writes often happens to me when I draw. I think it's because I chew on the end of the pen. Before I know it, that ink is everywhere. This is where you say to yourself, "Can any idiot be a syndicated cartoonist?" And I answer, "Most definitely."

Panel 1: HEY, STEPH, WERE YOU ALIVE DURING WORLD WAR TWO? / ARE YOU NUTS? THAT WAR ENDED 23 YEARS BEFORE I WAS BORN.

Panel 2: I KNOW. I'M JUST SAYING IT FOR PERSPECTIVE. / PERSPECTIVE ON WHAT?

Panel 3: THE FACT THAT YOUR PROM WAS 34 YEARS AGO.

Panel 4: THEN HE GUZZLED RUM AND CRIED.

To make matters worse, my prom date left me for another guy. I need more rum.

Panel 1: HEY, GOAT, WHERE WERE YOU LAST WEEKEND? / I WENT TO A WRITERS RETREAT.

Panel 2: RUN! RUN! WRITING'S TOO HARD!! / WRITERS

Panel 3: I'D GIVE UP, TOO. / I'M SO CONFUSED.

I've been to one writers' conference, and holy $#%#, those guys drink more than cartoonists.

Whenever my wife hosts big parties at our house, I always volunteer to be the bartender. That way I can cut off any conversation by telling someone I have to go make drinks. Plus, I'm being useful. So it's a win-win for everyone involved.

I get rid of my anger by yelling at people when I drive. It's like meditation, but more satisfying.

One time at a stop on one of my book tours, I told people to bring gin if they wanted their books signed. I was only kidding, but a bunch of very generous people brought me huge bottles of gin. The truth was that I couldn't fly to the next city with all that gin, so I had to give it to the employees of the bookstore. They did not object.

The weather service should provide dumbnado warnings.

I like drawing the earth because it gives me a chance to use my stencil. I am very fond of my stencil.

9/8

Ironically, less than a month after this strip, I got a letter from a United States senator (see the 9/10/19 strip).

I screwed this one up. I should have said "leap day" instead of "leap year." That way, it would have been clearer that Pig was picking the one day that only occurs every four years. Instead, "leap year" makes it seem like he is picking the entire year, which sort of kills the joke. So send your complaints to my editor, Reed Jackson, at: Reed Jackson Should Have Caught This One, c/o Andrews McMeel Universal, 1130 Walnut Street, Kansas City, MO 64106.

I maybe still have an AOL email address. And an iPhone 5. But I'll deny it if confronted.

158

This is the Time Lady's only other appearance in the strip. I really do need to bring her back.

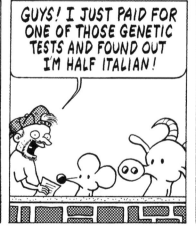

This strip resulted in a nice letter from the longest-serving United States senator—Patrick Leahy of Vermont *(see letter on next page)*. I must have met his grandson at a book signing.

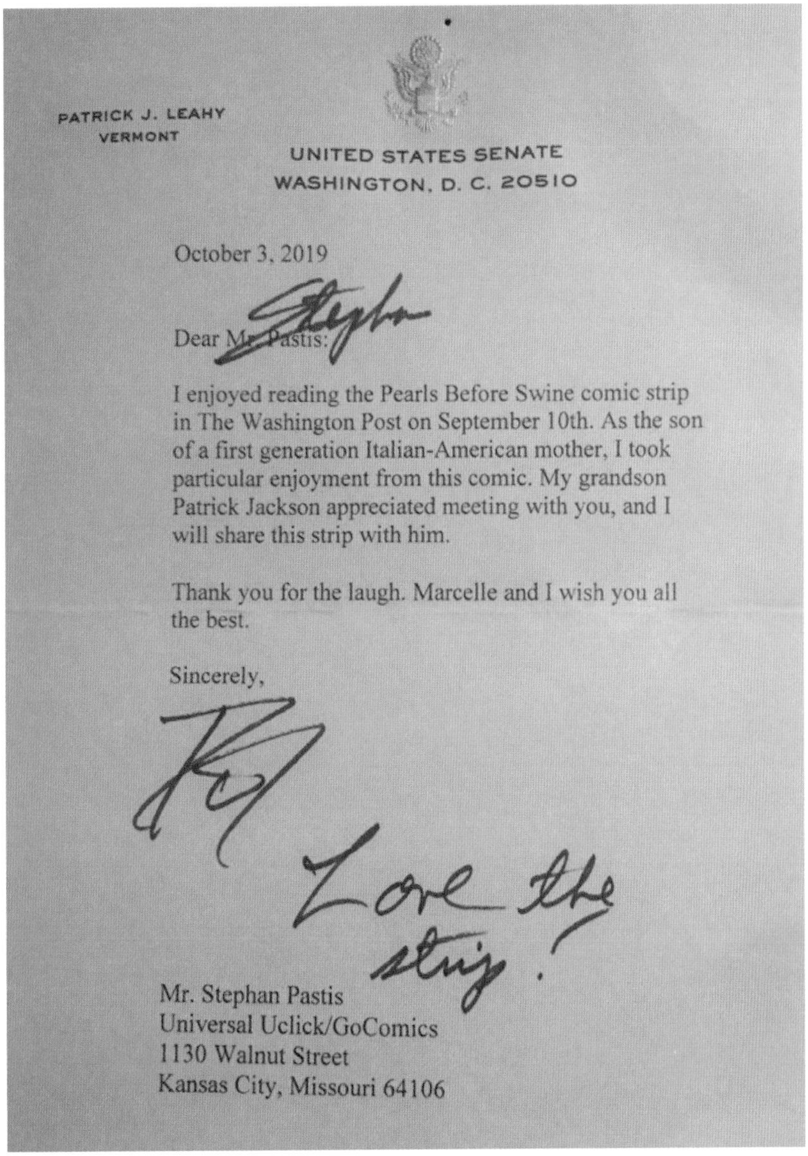

PATRICK J. LEAHY
VERMONT

UNITED STATES SENATE
WASHINGTON, D. C. 20510

October 3, 2019

Dear ~~Mr. Pastis:~~ Stephan

I enjoyed reading the Pearls Before Swine comic strip in The Washington Post on September 10th. As the son of a first generation Italian-American mother, I took particular enjoyment from this comic. My grandson Patrick Jackson appreciated meeting with you, and I will share this strip with him.

Thank you for the laugh. Marcelle and I wish you all the best.

Sincerely,

PJL

Love the strip!

Mr. Stephan Pastis
Universal Uclick/GoComics
1130 Walnut Street
Kansas City, Missouri 64106

Fun Fact: The Russian writer Alexander Pushkin got into at least 25 duels in his lifetime, the last of which was fatal. That's a big reason why I avoid dueling.

Yet another legacy of my living in Portland, Oregon, during the summer of 2018. These paper straws were everywhere. And they truly didn't work.

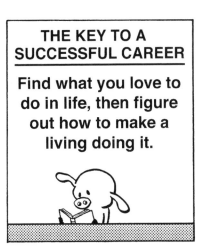

THE KEY TO A SUCCESSFUL CAREER

Find what you love to do in life, then figure out how to make a living doing it.

I love to sleep.

Pay me.

THIS WILL BE SO MUCH BETTER THAN WORKING.

I really feel fortunate to be doing what I love. I look forward to Mondays just as much as I do to Fridays or Saturdays.

HOW YOU THINK LIFE WILL BE WHEN YOU'RE YOUNG, AS EXPLAINED BY AN AMUSEMENT PARK...

WHEEEEEEEE

HOW LIFE TURNS OUT...

OHHH GAWWWWD

YOU LEFT OUT ALL THOSE CARNIVAL GAMES YOU CAN'T WIN.

ERRRGHH... WHY WON'T THE RING STAY ON THE BOTTLE?!

When my daughter, Julia, was really little, I would take her on the carousel ride at a park here in Santa Rosa. She would pick the most graceful horse that rose up and down, and I would get a dumb bench that didn't move at all. She was the most inconsiderate three-year-old I've ever met.

RESUME

WELL, LOOK AT YOU PREPARING TO GET A JOB INSTEAD OF SITTING AROUND ALL DAY DRINKING BEER. BUT JUST SO YOU KNOW, RÉSUMÉ HAS ACCENTS OVER BOTH THE 'E's.

WRITE WRITE WRITE

RESUME DRINKING BEER AFTER GOAT LEAVES

Note how Pig has a soft drink instead of the usual coffee mug. That's how I keep the strip hip and fresh.

Lately, I've taken to drawing the panel boxes with sloppier, hand-drawn lines. My editor, Reed Jackson, doesn't like it. But I think we've established what I think of Reed Jackson.

I wrote a kids' book series called *Timmy Failure*. I loved doing it, but I have a bit more creative freedom with the comic strip.

A tribute to my cartooning hero, Charles Schulz. The first couple panels are actual dialogue from a *Peanuts* strip.

I enjoyed drawing the third panel far too much.

I've rented Airbnbs where the Wi-Fi password is almost this long. It's really rather ridiculous.

I told you—I *really* like using my stencil.

I had the worst flying experience of my life in late 2018 when a snowstorm in Newark, New Jersey, caused me to be stuck in a grounded plane for 10 hours. Just Google "Stephan Pastis" and "United Airlines" to read about it.

Dear Me...

Stop doing things that torpedo my life.

You're far too good at it.

I'M HOPING ME'S LISTENING.

Me rarely listens.

HEY, KOKO KOALA... HOW GOES IT?

NOT GOOD. BEEN TRYING TO GET A JOB IN THAT FACTORY DOWNTOWN. BUT SO FAR, NOTHING.

I BET YOU'D BE GREAT AT CHECKING PRODUCTS AS THEY COME OFF THE LINE.

YOU THINK?

SURE. KOALATY CONTROL.

I WILL HIT YOU DOWN UNDER.

Hey, that's not a bad koala. Much better than my Marvin Gaye.

HEY, RAT, ARE YOU WALKING OVER TO THE CAFE TODAY?

I DON'T KNOW. LET ME CHECK THE FORECAST.

Chance of scattered idiots with occasional gusts of moron.

NEW WEATHER APP?

NEW 'WHETHER I CAN TOLERATE PEOPLE' APP.

VOCAB QUIZ

ENGLISH 1B

First, put a guy in a room that is lit.

Then *muss* up his hair. See what happens.

NOT THE DEFINITION OF 'LITMUS TEST.'

ENGLISH IS THE HARDEST CLASS EVER.

English 1B was a class I took in college. The professor xeroxed one of my papers to show the rest of the class how NOT to write an opening paragraph. But now I've published something like 50 books and have six *New York Times* bestsellers. So take that, you peckerhead.

TIP O' THE DAY

Whatever you do in life, give 110%

Why do I say that?

BECAUSE YOU ARE BAD AT MATH.

SOMEONE HAD TO TELL YOU.

RAT...YOU AND ME NEED TO TALK.

WHAT NOW, NEIGHBOR BOB?

YOU'RE USING YOUR LEAF BLOWER ON SATURDAY MORNINGS AT 8 A.M.

SO?

SO YOU HAVE NO LEAVES.

I DIDN'T THINK HE'D NOTICE.

DID YOU TELL HIM YOU JUST LIKE THE SOUND?

I love the idea of a guy walking around with a leaf blower for no other reason than he likes the sound.

Maybe I should write to my pen pal, Patrick Leahy, about this.

I did everything here except retire young and have nice kids. Mine are mean and petty and call me names.

Okay, this really is a thing. I always have to cover my exposed shoulder when I sleep (I sleep on my side, so it's the shoulder not touching the mattress). If I don't, something bad will happen.

HEY THERE, RAT... HOW ARE YOU?

I'M ALWAYS ANGRY AND I FEAR DEATH.

'FINE' IS A COMMONLY ACCEPTED ANSWER.

OH, AND I'M TIRED OF STUPID PEOPLE RUNNING EVERYTHING.

I know people who really do treat "How are you?" as an actual question and answer with a litany of complaints. So now I just say, "Hi."

SELF IMPROVEMENT QUIZ
To truly be happy, one must be able to answer "yes" to the following question: Are you being the best you you can be?

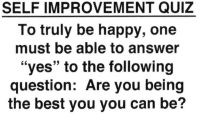

How do you answer that question?

Yes!

Explain:
God didn't give me much to work with.

NO WONDER I'M SO HAPPY.

WHAT ARE YOU DOING, PIG?

STANDING BEHIND MY PAL WHITNEY WHILE SHE'S ON THIS LADDER. WHIT'S AFRAID SHE MIGHT FALL.

THAT'S NICE OF YOU.

YEAH...HEY, COME STAND OVER HERE SO I CAN TELL YOU SOMETHING.

TELL ME WHAT?

THAT I'M AT WHIT'S END WITH YOU.

DITTO.

When I was a little kid, I went to a Houston Astros spring training game, and after it was over, a player named Denny Walling gave me his bat. It was about the most exciting thing that had ever happened to me.

173

Hey, two straight strips with baseball bats. Clearly, Denny Walling had a profound impact on me.

They should be more concerned that it's grown arms and legs.

The diner that Rat and Pig and Goat spend half their lives in has never had a name. Anyone have suggestions?

I really do wear a baseball cap pretty much all the time. Though it's rarely backwards.

I think someone should play a company's jingle nonstop in the CEO's office to see how he or she likes it.

I really live to travel. Some of the cooler places I've been to include India, Japan, Vietnam, Peru, Colombia, Australia, Afghanistan, and Iraq, as well as most of the countries in Europe. One day I hope to write a travel book.

No Knicks fan complained. Those poor people.

When I quit being a lawyer to become a cartoonist, my mom asked, "Do you have a plan B if this doesn't work out?" And I answered, "Nope."

This is what happens whenever I buy anything and have to assemble it.

DICTIONARY

Social:

Enjoying the company of others.

Social media:

Staring at an electronic device by yourself.

SOMETHING'S BEEN MISNAMED.

According to my phone, I spent *27 HOURS AND 42 MINUTES* on my phone last week. Please, God, tell me that's not true.

WHAT ARE YOU DOING?

DRINKING A COKE.

IT'S NINE IN THE MORNING. YOU CAN'T DRINK A COKE AT NINE IN THE MORNING.

WHO SAYS?

IT'S ACTUALLY A LAW.

I NEED TO STAY BETTER INFORMED.

YOU DO.

IF ONLY HE HAD WAITED 'TIL NOON.

When I was in Vietnam, I went to this restaurant that President Obama went to and ordered the exact same meal he did, which also included a beer. But it was 8:30 a.m. when I was there, which seemed much too early to start drinking. So I did the right thing and had three.

HEY GOAT... I MADE YOU A 'THINKING OF YOU' CARD.

WELL, THAT WAS THOUGHTFUL.

Thinking of you... Makes me sad.

MAYBE THINK OF OTHERS NEXT TIME.

THANKS. YOUR LIFE WAS REALLY BRINGING ME DOWN.

179

This was a little experiment in only using color on part of the cityscape panels. I like the way it came out.

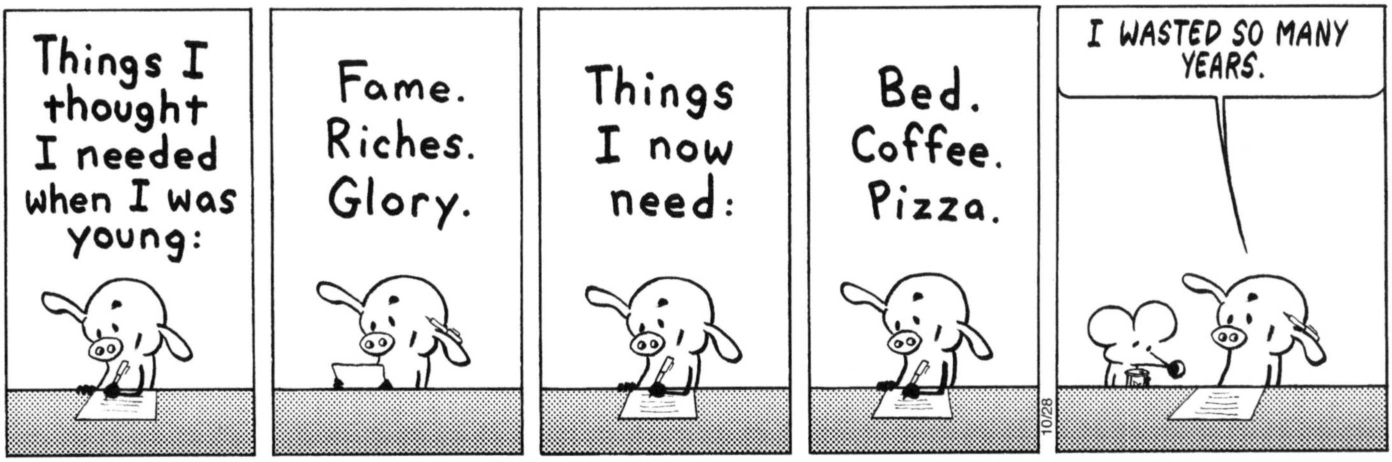
Things I thought I needed when I was young:
Fame. Riches. Glory.
Things I now need:
Bed. Coffee. Pizza.
10/28
I WASTED SO MANY YEARS.

I've noticed that if I drink more than two cups of coffee, my hands shake a bit too much to draw the strip. I notice it especially when I letter the dialogue. So on drawing days, I try to keep it to one or two cups.

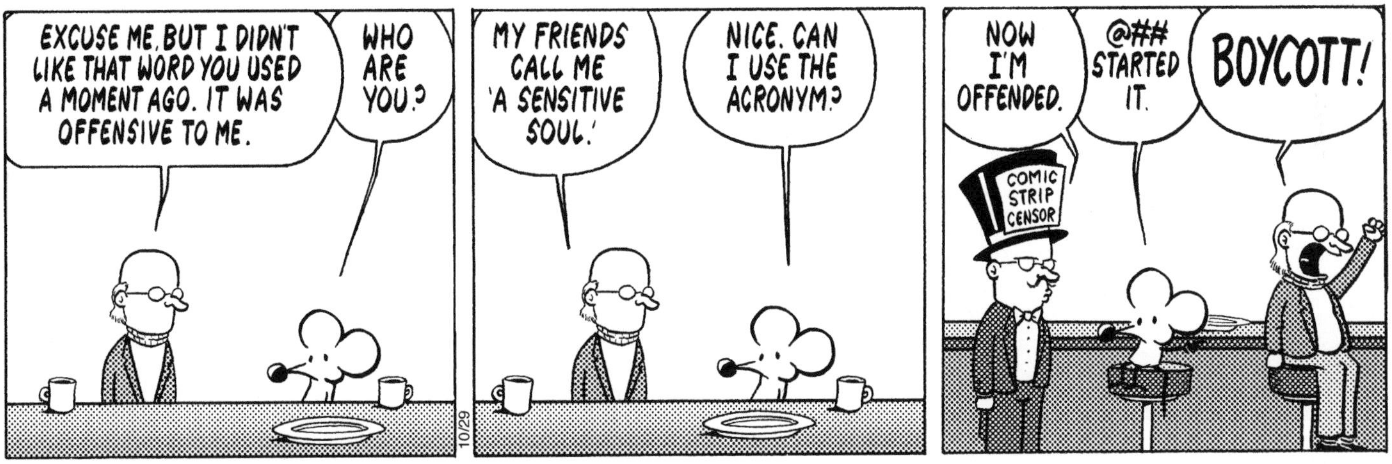
EXCUSE ME, BUT I DIDN'T LIKE THAT WORD YOU USED A MOMENT AGO. IT WAS OFFENSIVE TO ME.
WHO ARE YOU?
10/29
MY FRIENDS CALL ME 'A SENSITIVE SOUL.'
NICE. CAN I USE THE ACRONYM?
NOW I'M OFFENDED.
@## STARTED IT.
BOYCOTT!
COMIC STRIP CENSOR

Another case where I could have spelled it "@$$," but went with "@##" so the word wasn't quite as obvious.

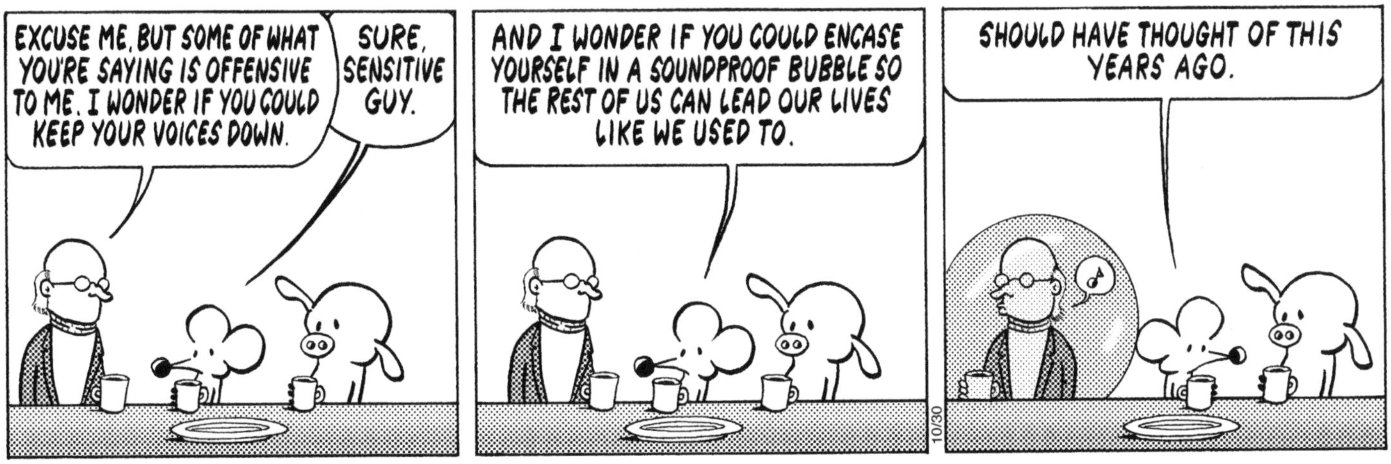
EXCUSE ME, BUT SOME OF WHAT YOU'RE SAYING IS OFFENSIVE TO ME. I WONDER IF YOU COULD KEEP YOUR VOICES DOWN.
SURE, SENSITIVE GUY.
AND I WONDER IF YOU COULD ENCASE YOURSELF IN A SOUNDPROOF BUBBLE SO THE REST OF US CAN LEAD OUR LIVES LIKE WE USED TO.
10/30
SHOULD HAVE THOUGHT OF THIS YEARS AGO.

The last line in the strip ("If you're not paying for journalism, you're paying for not having journalism.") became very popular among journalists on social media. I believe one newspaper even turned it into a T-shirt.

I think I have OCD as well. For example, I can't start drawing the strip if I can see the Kleenex sticking out of the nearby Kleenex box. So the first thing I always do is tuck it back in.

My wife and I recently played a game of Jenga that had giant, foot-long blocks. It was really fun. Until she won. Then my whole day was ruined.

I recently watched a documentary called *The Social Dilemma* which discussed the addictive properties of social media. It was pretty eye-opening.

All my human characters have very big noses. That second panel looks like a roomful of Pinocchios.

I have never been to any of my high school reunions. So in my mind, all of my classmates are still 18.

I am generally leery of any restaurant's signature dish, because it tends to be a bit overhyped. That said, I recently went to a restaurant in Munich that supposedly has the world's best pork schnitzel, and it was so good I almost wept.

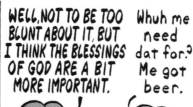
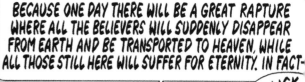

I like that the kindest thing Larry can think to do is donate beer to orphans.

Last year I traveled to the country of Slovakia. One late night, I was drinking and really wanted to find an open pizza place. Eventually I found one and noticed the chef sitting on the front stoop. Just as I looked at him, he picked his nose.

I went home hungry.

Sometimes cyclists make it far too easy to make fun of them.

Mob O' Snobs is pretty catchy.

I recently noticed that my Twitter account is followed by Magnus Carlsen, who is the chess champion of the world and has been for many years. He's a genius, so that must make me a genius.

The editor of this book, Lucas Wetzel, informs me that my logic in the comment above makes no sense. But he's not a genius like me and Magnus. So me and Magnus will ignore him.

This may be a good time to mention that my Twitter account is followed by fellow genius Magnus Carlsen.

My Aunt Leah used to have a magnet like this on her refrigerator. It said, "Mom's mood is . . ." And then you could flip the bottom of it to say "GOOD" or "BAD." I always turned it to "BAD."

Regarding that same Aunt Leah, I once went running to her house to play with my cousins (her kids), and as I ran, a candy I was chewing on got lodged in my throat. She saw I was choking and hit me over the back, probably saving my life. So I really should have been nicer about the whole magnet thing.

190

This really is what I do at parties. I go right to the host's bookshelves and try to find good authors I don't know. Then my wife, Staci, grabs me and tells me I have to talk to actual living people.

I just realized I forgot to draw Pigita's ears here. One would think I would be more adept at that after 20 years of drawing the strip. But one would be wrong.

In a weird way, this sort of foreshadows what would happen just a few months later with the pandemic.

192

Believe it or not, I had an ulcer when I was a little kid. Maybe Little League was causing great personal stress.

My wife refuses to buy Apple products for just this reason. Though that's the same wife who says it's polite to talk to other people at parties. So that makes me question her judgment.

Stephan's true-life confession: My wife buys most of my clothes. Because my judgment is even worse than hers.

This is doubly true of chili cheese fries. You cannot leave a single one on the plate. Though I draw the line at eating the cheese that gets stuck to the napkin.

The name of the café where Rat works, Joe's Roastery, is loosely based on a café called Calistoga Roastery in Calistoga, California, where I used to write the strip. If you go there, you will see many original *Pearls* strips on the wall.

I think the thing I'm best at in life is playing *Boggle With Friends* on my phone. And no, it's not sad.

I don't draw as many Guard Duck strips as I used to. I need to spend more time doing Guard Duck strips and less time playing *Boggle With Friends*.

I once got so high in Portland, Oregon, that I was unable to order cheese at a deli. Let that be a lesson, kids.

My problem is that I think that even when I'm sober.

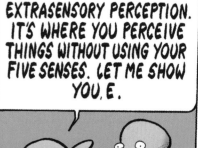

12/8

My wife is such a bad speller that when she sings this song, it comes out, "R-E-S-C-E-P-T, find out what it means to me."

 FOR THE SECOND TIME IN THREE YEARS, THE COUNTY I LIVE IN—SONOMA COUNTY, CALIFORNIA—HAS SUFFERED THROUGH MASSIVE FIRES.

 BUT THROUGHOUT IT ALL, WE WERE PROTECTED BY FIREFIGHTERS. PEOPLE WHO RACED TOWARD THE FIRE WHILE WE RACED AWAY, RISKING THEIR LIVES FOR PEOPLE THEY OFTEN DON'T EVEN KNOW.

 SO WHILE THE TERM 'HERO' IS SOMETIMES USED FOR ANY ACTOR OR ATHLETE WE MAY LIKE, LET'S APPLY THE WORD TO THE PEOPLE WHO REALLY ARE.

 THANK YOU. JUST DOING MY JOB.

And sadly, this year marked the third fire we've had in four years. The fire came within two miles of the studio where I'm writing this.

 DID YOU HEAR ABOUT THIS GUY WHO WAS KIDNAPPED?

 IS HE A KID? NO.

 WAS HE NAPPING? NO.

 EXPLAIN ENGLISH TO ME AGAIN. FINE, HE WAS MAN-NABBED.

 HEY, YOU'RE THE DRIVER WHO STOPPED AT THAT CROSSWALK FOR ME. YEP. NO PROBLEM.

 YES THERE IS. BECAUSE NEXT TIME YOU NEED TO STOP 30 FEET FROM THE CROSSWALK SO I FEEL COMFORTABLE WHILE I WALK AS SLOWLY AS I WANT AND OCCASIONALLY CHECK MY TEXTS.

 FASCIST PEDESTRIAN GUY. OUR NEWEST CHARACTER. OH, HELL NO. A DEAR FRIEND OF MINE.

No pedestrians complained, proving that cyclists really are the most easily offended group out there.

Panel 1: Dear Cable News People, Thank you for your insightful coverage of that big hurricane.

Panel 2: What I found especially informative was the part where your reporter stood in the wind.

Panel 3: I did not know that when you stand in the wind, it blows on you.

Panel 4: I'M HOPING THEY RECOGNIZE SARCASM. / SO *THAT'S* WHY HIS HAIR MOVES.

Sometimes you can do a strip like this one and then an actual hurricane happens that same day in the news, making it look like you're purposely making light of that day's event. So I made sure to run this strip in December, which is outside of the normal hurricane season.

Panel 1: HELLO? / HI...IS RICHARD THERE?

Panel 2: YEAH. THIS IS HIM. / OH, GREAT. WE JUST FINISHED PAINTING YOUR PORSCHE AND WERE WONDERING IF YOU NEED US TO DO ANYTHING ELSE.

Panel 3: YEAH. GIMME POLKA DOTS ON THE SIDES.

Panel 4: SOME PEOPLE JUST SAY 'WRONG NUMBER.' / MORE FUN MY WAY.

I really did this the other day. A guy called asking if I wanted him to touch up the paint in the den. Instead of telling him he had the wrong number, I told him I'd like to just knock out the entire wall. A long silence followed.

Panel 1: DO YOU THINK IT'S WEIRD THAT I SEND EMAILS TO MYSELF TO REMIND ME OF STUFF I HAVE TO DO? / WHY IS THAT WEIRD?

Panel 2: BECAUSE WHEN I GET THEM, I MARK THEM AS SPAM.

Panel 3: THAT CHANGES THINGS. / I WISH MYSELF WOULD STOP BUGGING ME.

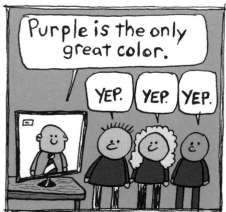

12/15

Don't listen to Pig. There are no better strips. So take that, *FoxTrot.*

This is really me. If a person has a lot of cats and there are rugs in the house, I'll be sneezing like a madman within 20 minutes.

I think about this sometimes. The fact is I don't actually know almost anyone's phone number anymore. So if there was an emergency and I didn't have my phone, I don't know how I'd reach them.

The only time I've ever felt fat was when I was in Vietnam waiting to take a zipline over a river. The guy in charge weighed me on a scale and informed me I was 201 pounds, one pound over the weight limit. I argued with him until he finally went and discussed it in Vietnamese with his boss, who agreed to let me ride. I'm fairly certain what the boss said was, "If fatty wants to die, let him die."

I did this strip after a friend told me he was always relieved seeing nuns on his flight. His theory was that God was less likely to let them die.

This strip really touched a lot of readers. As a cartoonist, if you don't do a lot of serious strips, the ones that *are* serious can really surprise people, thereby making a bigger impact.

Fun Fact: Growing up, I got to meet the actor who played Mike Brady (the dad) on *The Brady Bunch*. He used to come into the restaurant where I worked in South Pasadena, California.

If you have an iPhone, you can now check this by going to Settings and then Screen Time. If you're anything like me, the information might shock you.

One time at a bar in New York City, I ordered a Long Island iced tea, which is a drink that has rum, gin, vodka, and tequila. It was very popular when I was in college. The bartender replied, "What are you, 12? Order something else."

I recently got in trouble with my homeowners association for leaving food out for the birds. I think it would have been okay if it was birdseed, but it was leftover meat loaf.

206

This strip turned out to be one of the most unwittingly prophetic I have ever written, as the following year (2020) was the year of the pandemic, where hundreds of thousands of people died and millions of people lost their jobs. I was constantly asked throughout the year what it was that made me write it, and the truth is I have no idea. It was just one of those strips that turned out to be uncannily predictive.

The sketchiest bar I have ever walked into was in Tucson, Arizona. Behind the bar were a bunch of video screens showing live shots of the parking lot. I asked the bartender why they had those, and he said, "Oh, people keep getting stabbed out there."

This is why page-a-day box calendars are so much better. You can tear off the page for each day and angrily throw it in the trash can. And yes, there is an annual *Pearls Before Swine* page-a-day calendar that you can buy.

I tried a kale smoothie the summer I was living in Portland. It was quite possibly the worst thing I have ever put in my mouth, and that includes the odd assortment of things I picked up off the ground when I was five.

Lately I have taken to walking two or three miles every day. I write strips as I walk and record them into my phone's voice memo app. To others, it probably just looks like I'm a loon talking to himself. Which is also true.

This strip was inspired by the partial destruction of my own town, Santa Rosa, which burned in October 2017. The fire came within two blocks of our house.

I can't see myself ever retiring. As long as I'm able, I want to get up every day and create.

I recently watched a documentary on HBO called *Class Action Park*, all about a now-defunct amusement park in New Jersey that was extraordinarily dangerous and included a wave pool that the employees nicknamed "The Grave Pool."

There is a bar in Austin, Texas, called The Tiniest Bar in Texas. I drew Rat on the bathroom wall, and the drawing stayed up there for years. (Not sure if it's still there, but feel free to check for me.)

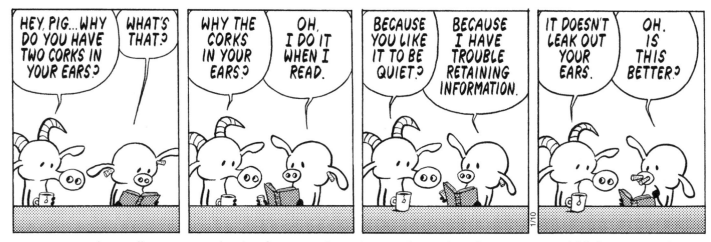

I once opened a really expensive bottle of wine, only to destroy the cork in the process and fill the wine with tiny bits of cork. No one thought it improved the taste.

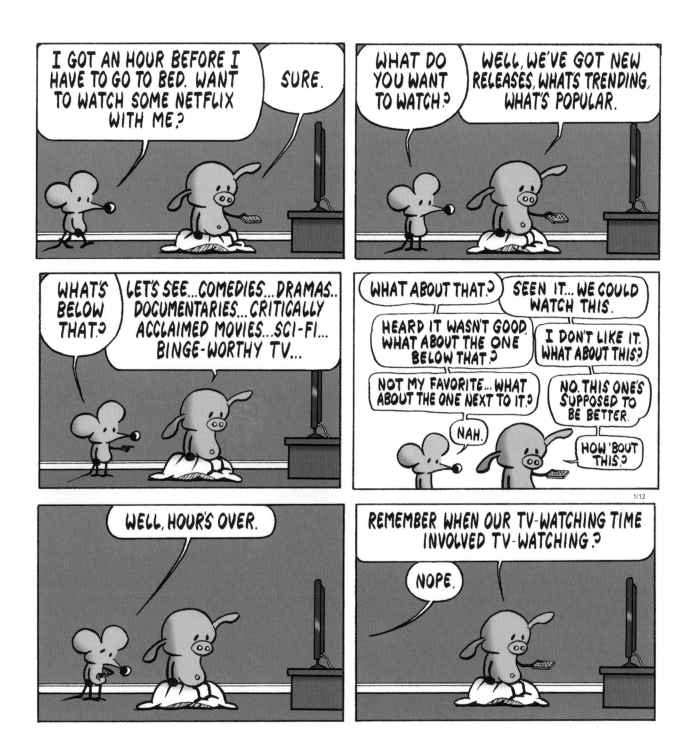

I really do spend more time picking movies on Netflix than I do watching movies on Netflix.

The song this is based on ("Lookin' for Love") is quite an earworm, and surely got stuck in many a reader's head for the rest of the day.

There's a bar in San Francisco called The Tonga Room where you can get rum-based drinks the size of your head. But the best part of the bar is the rainstorm that occurs in the center of the bar every 30 minutes. Then again, I may have just imagined that.

I actually did this one day and immediately thought, "Who's that tired-looking old guy staring at me?"

My daughter, Julia, takes craaaazy-hard calculus classes. I help by walking past her, pointing at different problems, and saying, "The answer is four."

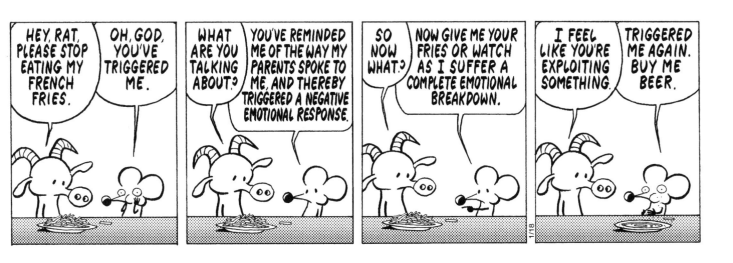

I colored this dog's fur like that of our late dog, Edee. My wife, Staci, printed out the strip and put it on her bulletin board.

Yet another legacy of my summer in Portland—a lot of these hipster types with jeans that squeezed their oompa loompas.

This is called "The Trolley Problem." Ninety percent of people choose to kill the one person and save the other five.

JOB QUESTIONNAIRE

Please identify an innate skill you have:

Speed.

Please explain:

When people do stupid things, I get mad **FAST**.

SOMEHOW I DIDN'T GET THE JOB.

HEY, RAT, I HAD A BUNCH OF RELIGIOUS FIGURINES, LIKE PRIESTS, BISHOPS, NUNS. ANYHOW, SOME OF THEM ARE NOW GONE. I'M WONDERING IF YOU TOOK ANY. NO OFFENSE.

NUN TAKEN.

I'm not in the habit of ending strips in silence. And if you got that pun, give yourself 10 *Pearls* points.

IF I WERE TO HAVE MY OWN NATION, I'D MAKE THE NATIONAL FLAG WHITE.

THE COLOR OF SURRENDER?

YES. SO OTHER ARMIES WOULD KNOW WE'RE NOT WARLIKE AND LAY DOWN THEIR ARMS.

AWW, THAT'S SO WONDERFUL.

AND THAT'S WHEN WE'D SHOOT THEM.

OKAY, WE'RE DONE.

TOO BAD IT WILL ONLY WORK ONCE.

From the Department of Only Tangentially Related Topics: When I was a lawyer, an associate of mine kept a loaded squirt gun in his office. He kept it there because he got tired of me taking a big wad of wet paper towels and hurling it over the top of his bathroom stall every morning. I always aimed right for his tie.

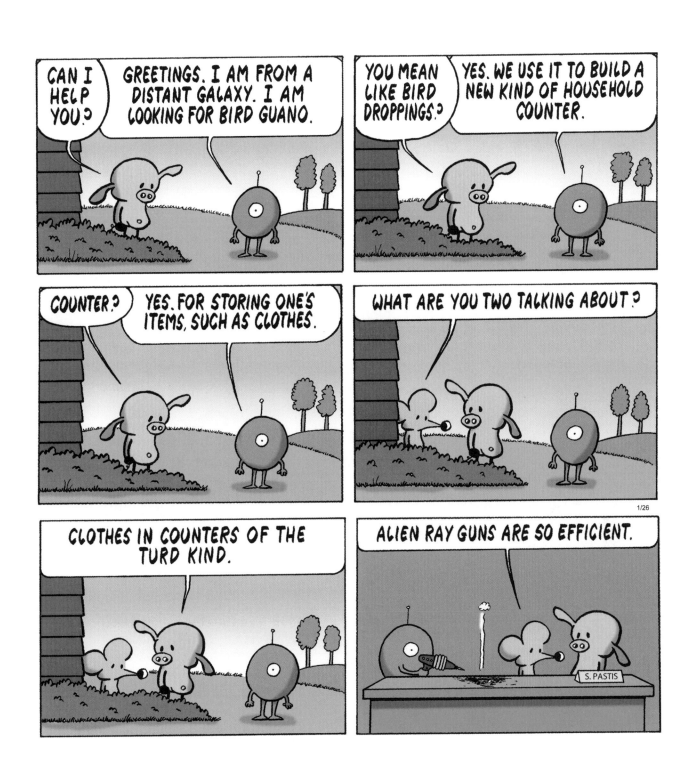

This strip is based on the movie title *Close Encounters of the Third Kind*, which was a huge hit when it came out in 1977.

I hate negotiating for anything. So when I travel to other countries and someone offers to sell me something that I'm supposed to haggle for, I lamely just say, "Is that your best price?" To which they always say, "Yes." And I then just give them the money.

I can be super talkative when I'm one-on-one with someone. But I get very quiet at any large gatherings.

As I write this, I'm planning a trip where I take the I-10 freeway from California to Florida and then return home on the I-40 (more or less). The trip I have in mind will cover 17 states. I want to then turn my adventures into a travel book.

Feel free to help these expressions catch on.

221

Speaking of which, someone once took a wildly unflattering photo of a very hungover me at a book signing in Helsinki, Finland, that has somehow become my profile photo on Wikipedia.

I do this night after night, and cannot appear to stop.

This is based on my best friend Emilio's indefensible decision to wear a beret on a trip we took together to Spokane, Washington. I remained friends with him only because I have no other friends and didn't want to be friendless.

No word on whether Emilio plans on wearing these along with his stupid beret.

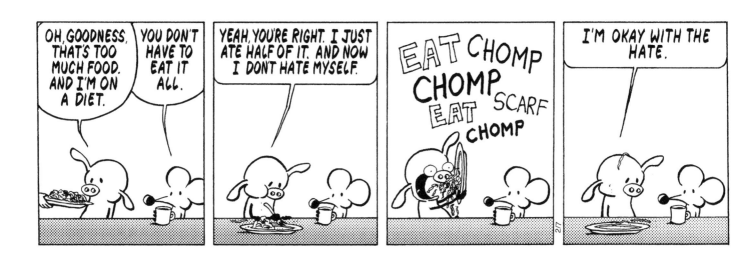

I recently heard of a job interview that a writer went to because he needed to earn money while trying to find a book publisher. When the interviewer asked him why he wanted the job, he thought for a moment and answered, "Actually, I don't."

This strip drew a bit of an angry reaction on social media, which is more or less the point the strip was trying to make. So I'm gonna say that makes me a genius. Just like Magnus Carlsen.

SO LET ME GET THIS STRAIGHT. YOU SPEND YOUR WHOLE LIFE TRYING TO ACCUMULATE KNOWLEDGE, GAIN INSIGHT, AND ATTAIN WISDOM, AND ONE DAY YOU DIE, AND IT ALL GOES AWAY.

YEP.

SO WHY NOT JUST SPEND YOUR WHOLE LIFE BEING STUPID AND EATING BONBONS?

YOU'VE JUST SUMMARIZED MY ENTIRE PHILOSOPHY OF LIFE!

SO IT TURNS OUT HE WAS THE SMART ONE ALL ALONG.

BONBONS GOOOOOD.

As I get older and more forgetful, I realize that this knowledge goes away while you're still living. Which is yet another reason to eat bonbons.

HEY, OLD MAN JOHNSON, HOW'S IT GOING?

NOT GOOD, PIG. BEING OLD IS TOUGH. LATELY, I'VE BECOME INCONTINENT.

WHAT ARE YOU DOING TO TAKE CARE OF THAT?

DEPENDS.

ON WHAT?

JUST TOLD YOU.

OLD PEOPLE MAKE NO SENSE.

I'M SO LOST, BUT I REALLY DON'T WANT TO ASK ANYONE FOR DIRECTIONS.

OH, PLEASE. WHAT'S STOPPING YOU?

EXCUSE ME...BUT... DO YOU KNOW THE WAY TO SAN JOSE?

DOO YOU KNOW THE WAY ♪ TO SAN JOSE... ♫

THAT'S WHAT.

IT WILL BE STUCK IN MY HEAD FOREVER.

Another song that I successfully implanted in everyone's head that day.

226

This really is what's supposed to happen to the earth in 7.5 billion years.

Spoiler alert.

I tried to build these things out of Campbell's soup cans when I was a kid and the only thing I could do when I tried to use them was smell tomato soup.

Our yard in Santa Rosa is filled with these huge boulders, as you will see from the photo on the next page. And please excuse the window glare. I was too lazy to walk outside.

HEY, LIFE COACH LARRY. HOW GOES IT?

GREAT. I HAD A SUPER PRODUCTIVE DAY. GOT IN A TEN-MILE RUN. DID ALL MY REPORTS FOR THE WEEK. ABOUT TO TAKE A GOURMET COOKING COURSE. HOW 'BOUT YOU?

I SLEPT SO MUCH THAT THE PILLOW MADE A PERMANENT CREASE ON MY FACE.

I DON'T IMPRESS LIFE COACH LARRY.

AACHOO!

BLESS ME.

THE EXPRESSION IS 'BLESS YOU.'

YEAH, BUT THAT'S STUPID.

WHY IS IT STUPID?

BECAUSE WHATEVER ILLNESS IT IS, YOU'VE ALREADY GOT IT, AND NOW WE'RE JUST ROOTING FOR ME.

SADLY, THAT'S LOGICAL.

THE TREND STARTS NOW!

By sheer accident, this strip was published just as the coronavirus pandemic began to explode in the US.

I DON'T REMEMBER ONE THING FROM BEFORE I WAS BORN. SO WHEN I DIE, DO I JUST RETURN TO THAT STATE?

MAYBE.

THEN WHAT WAS ALL THIS FOR?

EATING DONUTS.

HE MAY BE ON TO SOMETHING.

While in Portland, I became addicted to donuts from a place called Blue Star Donuts. And by mentioning them here, I believe I have earned a year's free supply.

While I did not get great art skills either, I am hoping I get free donuts from Blue Star. Specifically, a year's supply.

If you are ever bored one day and own an iPhone, ask Siri, "What is zero divided by zero?" You get a great answer.

2/23

Any similarity to the tight Lycra suits worn by cyclists is purely coincidental.

My life of sloth better include free donuts from Blue Star Donuts.

Although a controversy on Twitter can appear very large and ubiquitous, recent studies show that only one in five Americans is a regular user.

That fly took far too long to draw, as did the flyswatter. Thus, they shall not be returning to my comic strip.

My nephew John was almost born on this day. Had he been, he would only be a quarter of his current age.

I really like the drawing of the judge in the second to last panel. It's funny how often loose sketches turn out better than neat, orderly drawings.

If you've learned anything from these comments, it should be that I really like using my stencil.

I often wonder what additional cool things we would have now if Steve Jobs had lived another 10 years.

BAD NEWS. WE HAVE SAVED ABSOLUTELY NO MONEY FOR THE FUTURE.

GOOD NEWS. THERE MAY NOT BE A FUTURE!

I KNEW IT WOULD ALL WORK OUT.

This one makes me laugh. I think I enjoy the darkest strips the most.

DON'T YOU WISH SOMETIMES THAT THERE WAS THIS MAGIC THING THAT COULD MAKE YOU FEEL BETTER ABOUT YOURSELF AND MAKE EVERYTHING IN LIFE OKAY?

YES.

IT'S CALLED A SIX-PACK.

I MEAN LONG TERM.

IT'S CALLED A KEG.

This was a pretty popular strip.

Dear Powers That Be in the Universe,

I have had more than my share of bad luck lately.

So maybe pick on someone else for a bit.

P.S. I can suggest names.

I ALWAYS TRY TO BE HELPFUL.

I am sad.

Sad because I am lonely.

Lonely because no one in the world wants me.

And when you don't feel wanted, you feel invisible.

I used to comfort myself by thinking of all the other unwanted people there must be.

But sometimes it feels like I'm the only one left.

Especially at the post office, where the government announces all those whose status has changed.

3/8

WANTED WANTED WANTED
WANTED WANTED WANTED

SIGH.

HEY, MORON, THEY'RE CRIMINALS.

AW, NUTS. WOMEN ALWAYS LIKE BAD BOYS.

I have stared at this strip for a solid five minutes and cannot think of a single witty or insightful thing to say. So I'll just use this space to say that for a cartoonist, I'm not that bad looking.

Happiness is a journey!

Which must mean my car is broken down by the side of the road.

ARE THERE TOW TRUCKS FOR THIS?

IF YOU CAN DIE AT ANY TIME, WHAT'S THE POINT OF EXERCISE?

EXERCISE ISN'T ONLY ABOUT LONGEVITY. IT'S ALSO ABOUT FEELING BETTER ON A DAY-TO-DAY BASIS.

I FEEL BETTER WHEN I EAT A BUCKET OF FRIED CHICKEN WASHED DOWN BY A SIX-PACK.

ENJOY YOUR SHORT LIFE.

ENJOY YOUR LONG, SUCKY ONE.

I've taken full advantage of the fact that I can now say "sucks" and "sucky" on the newspaper comics page.

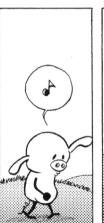

DAFFODILS! THE FIRST SIGN OF SPRING! YOU'VE BEEN DORMANT FOR SO LONG. LET ME FILL YOU IN ON EVERYTHING THAT'S BEEN HAPPENING IN THE WORLD!

THEY WENT BACK INTO THE GROUND.

My wife, Staci, has planted these all over the ground around our driveway. I've only run over six of them.

I really only use social media to post strips, mostly because I don't think people want to hear my opinions on things. Although I will say right here that I think it's fine to put ketchup on hot dogs.

Originally I was going to make this into a weeklong series of strips, but after drawing just one, I never followed through on doing more.

240

When I was in Oslo, Norway, I took a photo of the original painting of *The Scream* and was immediately reprimanded by a guard who told me that was not allowed. I wanted to argue, but didn't want to strain US/Norwegian relations.

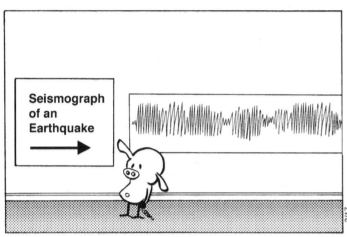

I was walking outside in Berkeley, California, during the big 6.9 earthquake that struck the Bay Area in October 1989. Because I was outside, I felt less of the effect. People who were indoors got a much scarier experience.

This might be a good time to tell Blue Star Donuts that my favorite donuts are the Buttermilk Old-Fashioned, the Chocolate Buttermilk Old-Fashioned, and the Cinnamon Sugar. And that I could eat a lot of them in a year.

I use the line in the second panel a lot. And oftentimes, it really does mean what it says in the third panel.

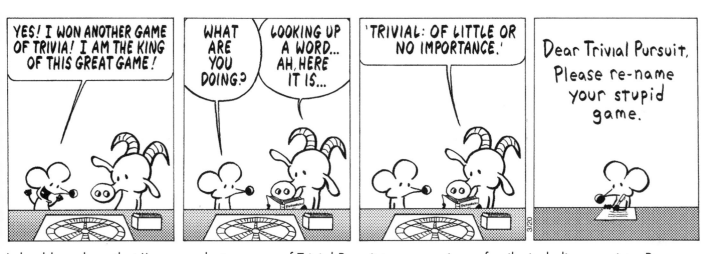

I should say here that I've never lost a game of Trivial Pursuit to anyone in my family, including my sister Penny, my niece Elenique, and my wife, Staci. All three of them would dispute that fact if they had their own published books to write comments in, but they don't, and that's too bad for them. So let me further add that I'm smarter than all three of them put together.

DANNY DONKEY WAS TIRED OF THE LONG WALK TO THE NEAREST LIQUOR STORE.

SO TIRED.

SO HE ATTENDED A CITY COUNCIL MEETING.

I propose to build three liquor stores in my neighborhood.

All the people in attendance booed.

BOO

BOOOO

BOOO

'As you see,' said the Mayor, 'That's a lot of boos you're getting. And if you ever come back, you'll be sure to get even more.'

SO DANNY DONKEY WENT HOME.

And one month later attended the next city council meeting.

I now propose to build SIX more liquor stores in my neighborhood.

3/22

'Didn't you hear what I said the last time?' said the Mayor.

'Yes,' said Danny... 'That if I came back, I would get even more booze!'

Danny was forcibly removed from the city council meeting.

Boot

CAN I BOO THIS STUPID STORY?

ONLY AT GREAT PERSONAL RISK.

THIS IS WHY I NEVER VOTE.

When I was growing up, my dad owned a liquor store in Covina, California. I used to love going there with him in the mornings because he would let me have all the packages of Topps baseball cards he had in stock (and then chew all the gum that came with it). Here is a picture of him in front of that liquor store in 1962.

Hey, a pun strip that didn't end with me being blamed. That feels nice.

Coconut is never a pleasant filling in anything. There are no exceptions to this rule.

VOCABULARY QUIZ

Define the word 'innate.'

YESTERDAY, NATE SWALLOWED AN ACORN.

IT IS NOW IN NATE.

SOME WORDS ARE EASIER TO FIGURE OUT THAN OTHERS.

I've never swallowed an acorn, but a girl in my seventh-grade class once got up in front of class and gave a speech on how she had gotten one lodged up her nose. No word on whether it's still there.

HEY, RAT...HOW COME YOU'RE NOT DRINKING BEER?

I REALIZED IT DOESN'T MAKE MY PROBLEMS GO AWAY. IT JUST MAKES THEM DISAPPEAR FOR A WHILE.

SO NOT A CURE FOR LIFE'S ILLS?

MORE OF A CRAPPY MAGIC SHOW.

THERE SHOULD BE REFUNDS.

LET'S DRINK TO FORGET THIS.

I can't do any magic tricks but I am able to do one card trick. It involves asking someone to pick a card from the deck of cards I'm holding. But the cards are facing me and so I can see the one they're picking. Which I guess isn't really a trick as much as it is an IQ test.

HEY, PIGITA, WANT TO GO OUT TONIGHT?

LET ME CHECK MY DAILY PLANNER... NOPE...LOOKS LIKE I'M BUSY TONIGHT.

HOW 'BOUT TOMORROW?

LET'S SEE...NOPE. BUSY EVERY NIGHT FOR THE NEXT NINE YEARS.

SHE IS SO DARN ORGANIZED.

And a nice uplifting note on which to end this treasury book. Hope you enjoyed the brilliant insights and startling revelations.

Loser No More!
(Bonus Section)

The highest award in American cartooning is called the Reuben, named for the cartoonist Rube Goldberg. It has been won by almost every legendary American cartoonist, from Walt Kelly to Charles Schulz to Garry Trudeau to Bill Watterson to Gary Larson.

Every year, three cartoonists (and now five) are nominated for the award by a vote of their peers. I was nominated for 10 straight years and lost every year.

Until 2019. When I finally won it. This was my acceptance speech.

So I'm in Albuquerque, New Mexico, and I'm behind the curtain about to go onstage and speak to a bunch of people, and the emcee is introducing me, going through my bio, and he says this:

"Stephan Pastis was nominated by his peers for the highest award in American cartooning—the Reuben—in 2009, 2010, 2011, 2012, 2013, 2014, and 2015, and won the award in each of those years."

So I knew the right thing to do when I went out there was to gently correct him and tell him that I had in fact *lost* all of those years. So when I went out there . . .

. . . I said nothing.

Who was I to ruin a good thing?

So while some of you may think this is my very first Reuben, the fact is that in certain parts of New Mexico, I have won eight.

So thank you to all the cartoonists I have had the privilege of being nominated with this year and every year.

Thank you to Amy Lago. Amy was the person who pulled *Pearls* out of a large submission stack and got me started.

Thank you to Ron O'Neal for selling the heck out of the strip.

Thank you to Dave Mace for the same.

And thank you to everybody at Universal, particularly John Glynn, for just being a legit kind person, through all the crises I manufacture and through all of those you cause.

But above all to my wife, Staci.

Staci has only come to two Reubens and I lost both years. And it was so disappointing. Because I knew, deep down—that she had jinxed me. But then I lost in succeeding years when she wasn't here, and I began to realize the truth—that she was jinxing me from home.

But here is the real truth and then we can get out of here.

As many a spouse or partner here in this room will tell you, living with a creative type is not easy.

Because we are moody, we are up, we are down, we are manic, we are boastful, we are mopey, we suck, we're great, we're unstable, we forget, we rage, we're nuts, and we quit, we un-quit, and quit again, and one person—one person that none of your peers ever sees—is there, in our homes, and on the phone, talking us off that ledge, telling us whatever truth or lie will get us through the night.

That person for me is Staci. Who happens to be here tonight.

So I'll say this directly to her:

First off, way to break the curse, babe.

Staci, when we had one small kid and another one on the way, and we were making real money from my job as a lawyer, I told you I wanted to quit that job, and take a chance on a career that had a very, very high failure rate. You never once questioned that. We never even had that discussion.

So in the years that followed, you, and only you, saw all of the highs and lows that no one else saw. Supporting me long after I had forfeited the right to ask.

So while others will see my name on that, I'll see yours.

Thank you to all of you, and to the NCS. I will take this home and put it with my other seven.

Huntington Beach, California
May 17, 2019

(Selfie of me and Staci taken in our hotel room before the event.)

Bonus
Bonus Section

After this book was completed, my editor, Lucas Wetzel, informed me that we still had some blank pages at the end of the book, which he felt very strongly we should fill with something. So on the next page you will find a photo of my hand.

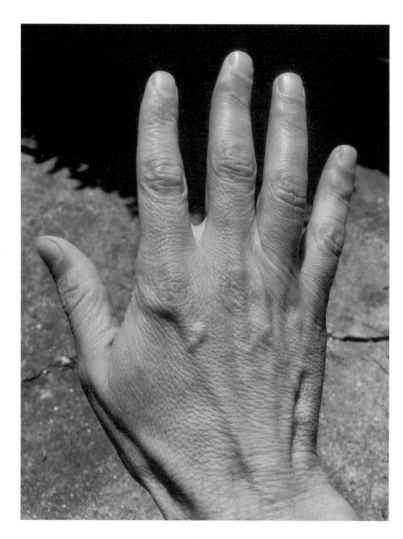

(My hand.)